D0145293

www.wadsworth.com

wadsworth.com is the World Wide Web site for Wadsworth and is your direct source to dozens of online resources.

At *wadsworth.com* you can find out about supplements, demonstration software, and student resources. You can also send email to many of our authors and preview new publications and exciting new technologies.

wadsworth.com
Changing the way the world learns®

Understanding Sexuality Research

Michael W. Wiederman
Columbia College

Wadsworth
Thomson Learning™

Australia • Canada • Mexico • Singapore • Spain • United Kingdom • United States

Senior Editor: Marianne Taflinger
Editorial Assistant: Suzanne Wood
Marketing Manager: Jenna Opp
Signing Rep: Lori Grebe
Project Editor: Pam Suwinsky
Print Buyer: April Reynolds
Permissions Editor: Joohee Lee
Production Services: Proof Positive/Farrowlyne Associates, Inc.

Cover Designer: Ross Carron
Cover Printer: Webcom
Compositor: Black Dot
Printer: Webcom

Printed in Canada

1   2   3   4   5   6   7   04   02   03   02   01

For permission to use material from this text, contact us by
Web: http://www.thomsonrights.com   Fax: 1-800-730-2215
Phone: 1-800-730-2214

Library of Congress Cataloging-in-Publication Data
Wiederman, Michael W.
   Understanding sexuality research / by Michael W. Wiederman.
      p. cm.
   Includes bibliographical references.
   ISBN 0-534-50958-4 (paper)
   1. Sexology—Research. I. Title.
   HQ60 .W54 2000
   306.7′072—dc21   00-025710

For more information, contact
Wadsworth/Thomson Learning
10 Davis Drive
Belmont, CA 94002-3098
USA
http://www.wadsworth.com

International Headquarters
Thomson Learning
International Division
290 Harbor Drive, 2nd Floor
Stamford, CT 06902-7477
USA

**UK/Europe/Middle East/South
Africa**
Thomson Learning
Berkshire House
168-173 High Holborn
London WC1V 7AA
United Kingdom

Asia
Thomson Learning
60 Albert Street #15-01
Albert Complex
Singapore 189969

Canada
Nelson Thomson Learning
1120 Birchmount Road
Toronto, Ontario M1K 5G4
Canada

Table of Contents

Preface

Having worked with numerous students on research projects involving the topic of sexuality, as well as having taught college courses on human sexuality, I am convinced that one of the most valuable aspects of being a student in these circumstances is learning how to be a more critical consumer of research findings. Learning how to think more like a scientist is a valuable enterprise— not necessarily to be able to conduct research, but rather to be able to more thoroughly evaluate research conducted by others.

Statements based on "the latest research" or a "recent survey" having to do with sexuality are common in the media. Over time some of these proclamations actually begin to contradict one another. How are people supposed to know what to believe or how much stock to place in findings from a particular research study?

This book is not about *what* to think, but rather about *how* to think. It is less about providing answers and more about learning how to ask good questions. Most of the principles covered in this book can be applied to any form of research on human behavior and attitudes, although all of the examples and applications have to do with research on human sexuality. The idea for the book came from my noticing that college textbooks on human sexuality include the obligatory chapter on research methods and pay lip service, at least, to becoming knowledgeable about how to evaluate research. Typically, after that early chapter, there is never again explicit mention of applying critical thinking skills to the research results that are presented.

In teaching human sexuality courses, I have found myself spending more time on research principles than most other topics presented in the textbooks. This was due partly to my belief that these principles were important to examine and learn. However, because the coverage of research issues in the textbooks seemed incomplete, I had to spend much class time discussing the basics of critical thinking as applied to research on human sexuality. This book is my attempt to supplement the material that is typically provided in the textbooks. As such, I have tried to keep the book brief enough so that its use as a supplementary text in college sexuality courses would be feasible. Just like any single example of research, this book is imperfect and incomplete. However, I hope you find it a useful guide to becoming a more savvy consumer of research on human sexuality.

A NOTE TO THE STUDENT

The large majority of facts and definitions you learn in your human sexuality course will be forgotten shortly after the exam or the end of the academic term. That is the reality of being asked to "learn" (memorize) a large amount of factual material in ways that often have little relevance to your life at present. However, if reading a book or being enrolled in a college course does not change you in a meaningful way, I think it is legitimate to question whether you actually *learned* anything.

I say this to make a case for your choosing to invest some of your time and energy in learning to understand research. If you do, you are liable to begin to view some of the statements people tell you and those you encounter from the media from a noticeably different perspective. Developing critical thinking about research will result in irreversible changes in how you approach and evaluate information. I believe this is what higher education is all about, and I hope you agree. Either way, I welcome your comments and suggestions.

A NOTE TO THE INSTRUCTOR

All of the information we ask or require students to learn is valuable, right? Otherwise, why should we bother? Unfortunately, I know from experience that the large majority of facts, figures, and definitions that students "learn" (memorize) for an exam are soon forgotten. As I look back on my own college transcript, I find there are certain courses listed, along with an A grade mind you, that I do not even remember taking! Hopefully, however, each of those courses shaped me in some ways that endured. Helping students to develop critical thinking skills is one such way to shape their futures and to make a noticeable difference in their lives.

Arguably, critical thinking is one of the most valuable skills we can foster in students, and one that is liable to serve them well for a lifetime (Halpern, 1998). Although we know more about human sexuality today than at any other point in history, our knowledge of human sexuality is incomplete in some areas and inaccurate in others. Only with the advantage of hindsight do we typically know where these areas are. This means that much of what we teach students today will become outdated or be proven wrong at some point in the future (probably within their lifetimes). Unfortunately, a college education does not automatically provide one with critical thinking skills (Tsui, 1999). I hope you consider the ultimate value and utility of spending a fair amount of course time to critical thinking about research and related issues. If you are reading this paragraph, chances are that I am preaching to the choir.

The first five chapters of this book lay out many of the most salient issues to consider when evaluating research on human sexuality. The remaining chapters briefly address thinking critically about research on particular topics that correspond with some of the major areas covered in textbooks on human sexuality. The purpose is to take the critical thinking principles learned at the start of the course and to apply them to some of the content areas. Each of these application chapters was written to stand independent of the other application chapters, so they can be read in any order (after having covered the first five chapters). Unfortunately, this strategy resulted in some redundancy of coverage in the application chapters, but I attempted to maintain each chapter's self-contained nature while minimizing any overlap.

At the end of each of the application chapters, I present three questions. These could be used for homework assignments, small group work in class, or class discussion. The questions are followed by a hypothetical case in which researchers conduct an empirical study on the topic at hand. I present these cases so that students can discuss and critique them, either alone, in small groups, or as a class. I also provide a list of six to eight relatively recent, relevant references to individual research studies that I believe would serve well as practice assignments. (Some of these studies are on InfoTrac, a service described below.) The primary criteria for selecting these studies were relevance to the topic, currentness, and representativeness of a wide variety of journals. The quality of the studies varies considerably; I do not rate or comment on these studies, since such evaluation is the students' objective. As with the questions and cases, students could tackle these selections individually, in small groups, or as a class.

Regardless of the periodical holdings at your particular institution, students can gain convenient access to journal and magazine articles on which to practice their newly developed critical thinking skills through *InfoTrac® College Edition,* available exclusively from Wadsworth/Thomson Learning. *InfoTrac® College Edition* is a fully searchable online library that includes the full text of articles from hundreds of scholarly and popular publications. Notably, *The Journal of Sex Research, Archives of Sexual Behavior, Canadian Journal of Sexuality, Sex Roles,* and *Family Planning Perspectives* are included among those periodicals. As students are most liable to encounter knowledge claims regarding sexuality from popular forms of media, practice evaluating presentations of sexuality information in popular magazines would be worthwhile. *InfoTrac® College Edition* includes such wide-ranging magazines as *Newsweek, American Health, Men's Health,* and *Essence.* The holdings in

InfoTrac® College Edition are updated daily, yet include articles up to four years old. You can give students in your course four month's access to this online library—24 hours a day, seven days a week, in the convenience of their own residence—if you choose to package *InfoTrac® College Edition* with this book.

I hope that you find the book useful, and I welcome your comments and suggestions.

ACKNOWLEDGMENTS

I wish to express appreciation to my mentors, Elizabeth Rice Allgeier and David L. Weis, for setting me on this path involving the study of human sexuality and to my good friend Kate Nicolai for providing the initial idea for this book as well as continued support and encouragement. Marianne Taflinger, Acquisition Editor at Wadsworth Publishing, also has my gratitude for her initial and ongoing enthusiasm for this book and future projects. Thanks also go to Allison Gilstrap and Nick Muchowicz for their comments on an earlier version of the first five chapters, and to Bernard Whitley, Jr., Dennis Hamel, and several anonymous reviewers whose comments resulted in marked improvements to the text.

Best regards,
Michael W. Wiederman, Ph.D.
Department of Human Relations
Columbia College
1301 Columbia College Drive
Columbia, SC 29203
Internet: mwiederman@colcacoll.edu

ABOUT THE AUTHOR

Michael Wiederman earned a B.S. in Clinical/Community Psychology from the University of Michigan—Flint (1989) and an M.A. (1991) and Ph.D. (1994) in Clinical Psychology from Bowling Green State University. He completed a predoctoral internship in the Department of Psychiatry and a postdoctoral fellowship in the eating disorders program at the University of Kansas School of Medicine—Wichita. Dr. Wiederman served as Assistant Editor and Consulting Editor for *The Journal of Sex Research*, has been an active member of the Society for the Scientific Study of Sexuality (SSSS), and has taught human sexuality courses at several colleges and universities. With regard to other books, Dr. Wiederman is coauthor (with Patricia Keith-Spiegel) of *The Complete Guide to Graduate School Admission: Psychology, Counseling, and Related Fields* (2nd ed.) and coeditor (with Bernard Whitely, Jr.) of the *Handbook for Conducting Research on Human Sexuality*. His research interests include sexual attitudes and experience, infidelity and jealousy, gender, personality, eating disorders, and body image.

one

THE QUESTIONS

I keep six honest serving men
They taught me all I knew:
Their names are *What* and *Why* and *When*
And *How* and *Where* and *Who*.
—Rudyard Kipling

Judge a man by his questions rather than by his answers.
—Voltaire

WHY UNDERSTANDING RESEARCH?

Why read a book about understanding research on human sexuality? Whether you are working your way through a college course on human sexuality or casually reading a magazine or watching a television program, you will encounter knowledge claims having to do with sexuality. These knowledge claims typically go something like, "Researchers found that men think about sex 3 (or 6, or 10) times more frequently than do women," or "HIV is spreading most rapidly among adults in their 20s." Such statements are knowledge claims in that the author is claiming to know something definite about the frequency of sexual fantasy among men compared to women or about the spread of HIV. As far as I know, these two examples are not necessarily accurate statements, but suppose I told you that they were. How would you go about evaluating their accuracy? Should you even question claims such as these?

The sexual fantasy example may not seem important and perhaps not worth your time to investigate or think about further. Likewise, depending on your current situation and behavior, you may not find the statement about the spread of HIV to be personally relevant. However, some knowledge claims might have strong implications for how you behave or how you make sense of your experience. Suppose that a newspaper headline contained a proclamation regarding the latest research on the proportion of individuals who have a certain sexually transmittable disease yet do not have symptoms, or a magazine article cited research on women's emotional well-being following an abortion, or a television program contained a reference to research on ethnic differences in the number of sexual partners. These knowledge claims could affect your decisions regarding your own behavior as well as your views of yourself and specific groups of people.

Sometimes knowledge claims regarding sexuality are used for political ends and are meant to affect your beliefs and behavior. Some individuals and groups are interested in swaying your opinion or gathering votes (or contributions) to support a particular political position. Common knowledge claims include issues such as abortion rights, sexuality education in schools, censorship of sexually explicit media, and marriage and parenthood among homosexual couples. In these cases, knowledge claims may be used in an attempt to paint a certain picture of reality. However, the individuals or groups making the knowledge claims are liable to choose the findings and bits of data they think best support their cases. The issue of the quality of those findings or data, and any findings and data that contradict their positions, is typically ignored.

Avoiding politically charged topics for the moment, consider an example of a knowledge claim that you probably have heard: Men reach their sexual peak in their late teens (age 18?), whereas women reach their sexual peak in their 30s (or later?). I have witnessed this knowledge claim being hauled out to explain everything from a particular woman's sexual interest in a younger man to women's general sexual dissatisfaction within marriage to parents' concern over the teenage boy their daughter is dating. This knowledge claim implies some inherent or biological difference between the sexes, such that men's sex drive has cooled by the time their female peers' sex drive is revving up and reaching its highest point. In reality, however, there is no evidence for such a biological sex difference (Baldwin & Baldwin, 1997).

The knowledge claim about men's and women's sexual peak derives from data Alfred Kinsey and his colleagues (1948, 1953) collected a half century ago. These researchers tabulated the total number of self-reported "sexual outlets" for each respondent per year—that is, the total number of orgasms or ejaculations each individual experienced through any means (e.g., masturbation, oral stimulation, vaginal or anal intercourse, erotic dreams). When these researchers graphed the total number of sexual outlets as a function of the age of the respondent, the line on the graph peaked (was highest) for men among those respondents who were in their late teens. For women, the graph peaked among those who were in their 30s.

It appears that the best explanation for this apparent sex difference has much more to do with what it meant to be a male or female raised in the United States during the early part of the 20th century than it does any physiological, hormonal, or anatomical sex difference. That is, the apparent difference in men's versus women's timing of the frequency of sexual outlets was primarily the result of greater social prohibitions placed on women compared with those placed on men with regard to being a "sexual" person, stimulating one's own genitals, and having sexual relationships other than within marriage (Baldwin & Baldwin, 1997). Much more recent data indicate that the frequency of sexual activity declines over the life span for both men and women, and men and women report very similar levels of sexual activity within each age group (Jasso, 1985; Robinson & Godbey, 1998).

If anything, some research indicates that, at least among married individuals, the decline in frequency of sexual activity may have more to do with gradual decreases in women's hormones than with men's hormonal levels (Udry,

Deven, & Coleman, 1982). Also, the original graphs upon which the knowledge claim was based were constructed to summarize data on large groups of people surveyed at a single point in time; they did not represent a participant's life course or changes over time. So, the data peaks did not necessarily correspond to peaks in sexual interest within an individual's life. Questioning the basis for knowledge claims about men and women experiencing different sexual peaks requires critical thinking.

WHAT IS CRITICAL THINKING?

Thinking critically about research means knowing the right questions to ask to assess the validity or accuracy of a knowledge claim. Many times there will not be anyone present (or the necessary information available) to adequately answer the questions you raise. However, stopping to ask the questions will lead you to be appropriately skeptical or cautious of particular knowledge claims (which are typically made with some sense of authority) until they can be substantiated. Note that thinking critically is not necessarily the same as criticizing someone or someone's research. Thinking critically about research leads to appreciation of the strengths as well as the weaknesses of a particular study. Rather than criticism, critical thinking requires curiosity and the ability to ask relevant questions and challenge the assumptions made by the author of a knowledge claim.

Critical thinking also requires taking a logical approach to understanding the topic, being careful to consider how our own emotions, beliefs, and biases, as well as those of others, can influence how research is conducted, data are gathered, and results are interpreted. Thinking critically about sexuality research involves separating facts from opinions and examining available evidence as objectively as possible. Using sound logic to draw conclusions from the evidence requires the ability to consider alternative explanations for the research findings. Might there be another explanation for the data other than the one that is provided or the one that seems obvious? Typically there are several alternative explanations or interpretations of any fact regarding human sexuality, and being a good critical thinker means being willing to accept that ultimate answers to questions about sexuality are not liable to be simple or clear-cut. Oftentimes a person is left with more questions than when he or she began studying a particular topic.

There are some questions worth asking of knowledge claims in behavioral and social sciences generally, and other questions that are more specific to research on human sexuality. Owing to the need to be brief, coverage in this book is focused on some of the most important questions and issues within sexuality research, with the ultimate goal of helping you become a more savvy consumer of research results. The hope is that, after working your way through this book, you will be able to more critically assess those knowledge claims you encounter, and perhaps even help educate those who are around you when such knowledge claims are made. The first step in the process is learning more about where knowledge claims originate.

WHO STUDIES SEXUALITY?

Because knowledge claims in sexual science are based on some form of data, our first question is, "Who is collecting the data?" When reporters, textbook authors, or classroom instructors begin a statement with "Scientists have found . . ." or "Researchers report . . .," it is easy to envision a colony of middle-aged adults (usually balding white men in white lab coats) who are secluded from the mundane lives of ordinary people. In reality, most research on human sexuality is conducted by university faculty members. Because these women and men have courses to teach, students to advise, committee meetings to attend, groceries to buy, families to care for, homes to keep up, and so forth, research actually occupies only a small portion of their time, attention, and personal identity.

In a book titled *The Sex Scientists* (Brannigan, Allgeier, & Allgeier, 1998), several faculty members share why they chose the field of sexuality science and describe some of their more interesting experiences. The book serves to reveal the human side of sexuality researchers and to take some of the mystery out of the profession. My purpose in stressing that sexuality researchers are humans with multiple roles is to emphasize that these professionals who collect the data upon which knowledge claims are based are less than perfect; they make mistakes, have varying abilities and levels of expertise, may have differing motives and personal biases, and ultimately conduct their research in more or less flawed ways, as do all researchers.

Unfortunately, when a science-based statement is ascribed to a professor or an authority figure in print, over the airwaves, or through cyberspace, it is easy to attach a great deal of accuracy and sanctity to the statement. This probably happens most often when the statement is found in a research report published in a scholarly journal, especially when the article also contains unfamiliar statistical symbols and references to statistical tests and procedures. It can be quite impressive. If something is published in a research journal or a college textbook, it must be accurate and above criticism, right?

It is important to recognize the motives behind sexuality research and the publishing of research journals. The primary motives of both researchers and publishers usually involve the desire to advance knowledge and to be a vital and respected part of that process. Those who conduct research on sexuality often do so with great enthusiasm and derive much satisfaction from their work. (Contrary to one stereotype, however, the stimulation involved in the

6 CHAPTER 1

process is intellectual and not sexual—unless your idea of an erotic evening involves studying anonymous questionnaires and columns of numbers in data files and statistical printouts.) There are important secondary motives, as well.

Untenured professors have to prove themselves worthy members of their profession, and a common way for them to do that is to publish the results of their research in scholarly journals. Sometimes research on sexuality is conducted with student collaborators for the primary benefit of the students (research experience and publication are advantageous when applying to graduate school or for a job). If the data were gathered by a magazine, such as in a reader survey, the primary motive may have more to do with generating some juicy findings in order to sell future issues than in advancing scientific knowledge. If the data were collected by an organization or agency, the primary motive might be to gather evidence to bolster its position on a particular policy issue or to legitimize its requests for funding from individuals or from the government. Secondary motives for publishing a journal also include maintaining the viability of the publication so that revenues from library and professional subscribers will continue to flow to the organization publishing the journal (money is indeed an aspect of the science process).

No one should assume that all research was conducted with objectivity and that all published research reports have met some "gold standard" of quality (Rosenthal, 1994). The process researchers have in place to ensure quality in published research is much like our country's legal system; it may be the best we have but it is far from perfect. Most (although not all) research journals publish only *peer-reviewed* manuscripts. This means that the article a researcher would like published is sent by the editor of the journal to other professionals who have expertise in the article's topic.

Typically there are two or three experts per manuscript who review it "blind"; that is, the names of the authors and their affiliations are removed from the manuscript before it is sent to the expert reviewers. This prevents any personal biases the reviewer might have about the authors from interfering with his or her objective assessment of the research. The reviewers (and editors) are almost always other university professors, each with their own courses, students, research, families, and so forth. Reviewers and editors have their own limitations with regard to knowledge and biases; hence the reason for having more than one reviewer per manuscript. Manuscripts that generally receive a positive evaluation by the reviewers and the editor are sent back to the author for revision (sometimes minor and sometimes major) before being placed in line for publication. The typical span of time from when a manuscript is initially sent to an editor and when it finally is printed in the journal runs from 18 to 24 months. Many times a research report is initially rejected by a journal, so it is revised before it is submitted to a second journal, where the entire review process starts again. By the time the research results appear in a scholarly journal, they are relatively old by science standards, and there is a good chance that the researchers who produced them have since completed other projects.

There are several journals whose primary purpose is to publish research on human sexuality (see Table 1). The result is a great deal of variation both within and across journals with regard to the quality of manuscripts published. Still, the purpose of peer review is to ensure some acceptable level of scientific rigor before research results are widely reported. A problem arises when research results find their way into mass media before those findings have been scrutinized in the peer review system. Frequently, results from the "latest study" or "most recent survey" appear in mass media outlets prior to having undergone review by other researchers. In these cases the public is left without any assurances that the research is scientifically sound. It may be that a particular study has a fatal flaw that knowledgeable reviewers evaluating the research would discover before it is submitted for publication, which would prevent the study from being published. If the findings have already been written about in newspapers or discussed on television, the flaw in the

TABLE 1.1	CURRENT JOURNALS WHOSE PRIMARY OBJECTIVE IS PUBLISHING RESEARCH ON HUMAN SEXUALITY

AIDS and Behavior

AIDS Care

AIDS Education & Prevention

AIDS Public Policy Journal

Archives of Sexual Behavior

Canadian Journal of Human Sexuality

Culture, Health & Sexuality

Journal of Gay, Lesbian, and Bisexual Identity

Journal of HIV/AIDS Prevention & Education for Adolescents and Children

Journal of Psychology and Human Sexuality

Journal of Sex Education and Therapy

Journal of Sex & Marital Therapy

Journal of Sexuality and Disability

Sexual Addiction & Compulsivity

Sexual and Marital Therapy

Sexual Dysfunction

Sexualities: Studies in Culture and Society

Sexuality and Disabilities

The Journal of Sex Research

research may never be reported. For this reason, more credibility should be afforded to research results that have been published in reputable scholarly journals, even if they are presented first on the evening news.

At this point, it may sound as though I am pessimistic about deriving anything of value from research on human sexuality. On the contrary, I have spent a fair amount of energy engaged in the process of conducting such research and writing about it (and reviewing others' research manuscripts submitted for possible publication). I, like many other scientists, believe that research is the best means we have for understanding human sexuality. Decades of sexuality research have resulted in many useful discoveries and a growing accumulation of knowledge. College textbooks in sexuality courses would not exist without the research that already has been conducted. However, as I am sure it is clear by now, researchers need to be critical consumers of data.

In the chapters that follow, you will examine particular aspects of sexuality research, learning the questions to ask to better evaluate the soundness of the research and the amount of credibility to attribute to the results. Each chapter contains specific examples similar to those you are liable to encounter. After you learn the basics of the research process and the critical questions to ask, you will examine research issues inherent in 10 different topical areas.

As you progress, it is important to remember that, just because a study has particular flaws, the research is neither necessarily worthless nor the results inaccurate. Even if seriously limited, some information on a sexuality topic is, in general, better than no information at all. Without research on human sexuality, all we are left with are personal beliefs, myths, and stereotypes.

Congratulations! You have taken the initial step in becoming a critical thinker about research on human sexuality. The next step involves considering the knowledge questions researchers are trying to answer.

WHAT ARE THE GOALS OF THE RESEARCH?

What are the goals of the research? Of course for each study there may be several answers to this question. Sometimes the goal is simply to discover and describe what exists. Such *descriptive* studies are conducted to determine the frequency of particular sexual behaviors or experiences, or to document public opinion about some sexuality issue. Sometimes the goal of research is to discover relationships among variables. For example, is there a relationship between age and sexual attitudes? A *correlational* study would answer this question. Sometimes the goal of research is to determine what causes or influences a particular behavior. Such *experimental* studies involve manipulating conditions to observe what effect, if any, the manipulation has on behavior.

Each of these types of research, and their strengths and weaknesses, will be examined later in this chapter. First, what is the best way to determine why a particular study was conducted? Does it matter?

WHY WAS THE RESEARCH CONDUCTED?

Often the reason for the research is contained in the hypothesis statement. A *hypothesis* is simply a research question, such as "Do men and women differ in their sexual attitudes?" or "What is the relationship between feelings of love for a sexual partner and the likelihood of using a condom?" Why is it important to consider the reason the research was conducted? Such statements tell the reader the primary focus of the research as well as what the researchers hoped to learn from their work. This information is helpful in evaluating whether the research design was adequate to answer the primary research questions and whether the writers are justified in their interpretation of their findings and the implications they draw from them. In a nutshell, the research questions the writers pose tell us what we can expect to learn from reading about the research and cues us into the aspects of the research we should examine with special attention.

Hypotheses or apparent reasons for the research also may tip us off with regard to possible agendas or biases the researchers have. Researchers are, after all, simply human and can be influenced by their own sexual beliefs and experiences. In Chapter 1 I mentioned the historic work of Alfred Kinsey and his colleagues. That team of researchers was among the first to attempt to empirically study human sexual behavior, at least on a large scale. However, others have questioned whether Kinsey's own sexual beliefs and practices might have colored the objectivity of his work (Jones, 1997). Although such concerns may have been overblown in this case (Bullough, 1998), they raise the possibility that researchers can be blinded to the ways in which their own opinions and experiences may shape how they approach a research topic.

For example, consider one published study of adolescents who had not experienced sexual intercourse. One of the stated research questions was "What reasons do abstinent adolescents give for not becoming sexually active?" (Blinn-Pike, 1999, p. 297). This research question is rather straight-forward and objective. However, in the introduction to the study, the author wrote extensively about the harm associated with teen sexual activity and the need to foster "resilient" youth who remain abstinent. To determine adoles-cents' reasons for abstinence, the researcher presented respondents with a list of 18 reasons and asked teens to indicate whether each was a reason he or she was sexually inactive. Given the personal beliefs the researcher revealed in her description of the study, it is not surprising that her list of reasons for abstinence did not include anything referring to "not having had the opportunity." Teens who would like to have had sexual intercourse but who have not simply because they lacked the opportunity were not given a way to express their opinions. The response choices the researcher con-structed may have been influenced by her personal assumptions about why teens would not have sexual intercourse (e.g., "waiting for marriage" or "fear of AIDS").

Where do we find a hypothesis statement? If we are reading a formal report of research, such as an article in a scholarly journal, finding a direct or indirect statement of the purpose or objective of the research is fairly easy. Convention dictates that the purpose of the research be stated in the abstract (found immediately before the body of the article) as well as somewhere near the end of the introduction section of the article (right before the details about the methods used). Sometimes, however, research hypotheses are not explic-itly stated and must be inferred from the framework the researcher provides for the report. For example, if the introduction to a study on teen sexual activ-ity is loaded with statistics and descriptions highlighting how harmful such activity is, we might assume that the researcher hoped to discover some infor-mation useful for curbing rather than enhancing teen sexual activity.

What if one hears about research findings on television or reads about them in a magazine, newspaper, or textbook? In these cases we are usually not told the reason or objective of the research, so it can be just as useful to turn our evaluative question around. Instead of asking why the research was conducted, we could ask, "What kind of research would one have to conduct to accurately arrive at that conclusion?" To answer that question we need to be familiar with the various types of research designs and the strengths and weaknesses of each.

KINDS OF RESEARCH

Descriptive studies are meant to describe the state of affairs with regard to a certain sexual behavior, experience, or attitude. Research designed to determine parents' attitudes toward their children's masturbation, the percentage of people who have had extramarital sex, or the frequency of oral sex among dating couples are all examples of descriptive studies. Descriptive studies cannot be used to determine anything about relationships among variables or what causes particular attitudes or behavior. However, research on any particular sexuality topic generally begins with descriptive studies that document that there is something that needs further study.

We say research is *experimental* when the researchers manipulate some variable(s) and examine the effect of that manipulation. For example, researchers interested in the effects of exposure to pornography on men's attitudes toward women might measure such attitudes in two groups: the first group was not exposed to any visual media, or perhaps only to media with non-sexual content, whereas the second group was shown a set amount of pornographic media. If participants in the study were randomly assigned to either of the two groups, then the researchers assume that they are similar in all aspects except exposure to pornography. If the two groups subsequently differ in their reported attitudes toward women, the researchers conclude that exposure to the pornography affected the men's attitudes.

One weakness of experimental research is that often the experimental manipulation does not match well with reality. In the current example, it is unlikely that the amount of exposure to pornographic media in the experiment would be anywhere close to the amount experienced by men who seek out pornography in their personal lives. Because the exposure to pornographic media in the experiment is limited, only one or a few particular film clips or photographs will be used. Are these representative of all pornographic films or photos that are available to consumers? Also, if the men are randomly assigned to the two experimental conditions, then many of the men who are exposed to the pornographic media are not men who would expose themselves to it outside of the research setting. The way these men are affected by the exposure to pornography may not mirror how men who seek out pornography in the real world would be affected.

Sometimes researchers are not able to perform random assignment of research participants, and they must make do with the groups available. For example, suppose researchers were interested in evaluating the effect of a therapy program on sexual dysfunction. In an experiment, people seeking treatment for a sexual problem would be randomly assigned to a treatment group or a control group that did not receive treatment. However, suppose that, as potential research participants telephoned a sex therapy clinic seeking help, the researchers were not allowed to deny treatment so that they could form a comparison group. Luckily for the researchers, at some point the clinic received more patients than can be treated at one time, so people calling after that point were put on a waiting list.

Now the researchers can examine the degree of improvement in sexual functioning between the patients receiving treatment and those waiting to receive treatment. Because one group is being treated differently than the other group, this type of study resembles an experiment. However, because there was no random assignment, this research design is referred to as *quasi-experimental*. Unfortunately, without random assignment to the two groups, the researchers cannot be sure that the groups are alike in all respects other than having received treatment. There is the possibility that differences in the rate of improvement between the two groups might be due to something other than treatment. Still, it is better to perform a quasi-experiment than no research at all.

In contrast to the experiment, most research on human sexuality is *correlational*; that is, variables are not manipulated, but rather the researchers measure at least two variables and examine relationships between them. The resulting correlation coefficient (abbreviated r) can range from -1.00 to 1.00. The presence or absence of a negative sign simply indicates the *direction* of the relationship between the two variables and has nothing to do with the strength of the relationship. A negative sign indicates that as the value of one variable increases, the value of the other variable decreases; whereas the absence of a negative sign indicates that as the value of one variable increases, the other increases as well. So, a correlation of $-.42$ actually indicates a stronger relationship between two variables than does a correlation of $.27$.

Returning to the earlier example, if the focus of research is possible relationships between exposure to pornography and men's attitudes toward women, the researchers might ask men to complete a questionnaire containing measures of pornography use (e.g., "How often during the past six months did you watch an 'adult,' or X-rated, video?") as well as attitudes toward women. To the extent that scores on the two measures are related, the researchers conclude that exposure to pornography *may* affect attitudes toward women.

When interpreting results of correlational research, conclusions as to cause and effect are speculative at best. All the researchers can say for sure is that the two variables appear to be related. However, because the researchers did not manipulate either variable, it is unknown which variable affects the other, or whether both are due to some other (third) variable or set of variables. In our current example, does exposure to pornography lead men to hold different attitudes toward women, or are men who hold particular attitudes toward women most likely to seek out pornography? Alternatively, perhaps men who are most religious happen to hold particular attitudes toward women *and* happen to be least likely to seek out pornography, so attitudes toward women and pornography use do not affect one another, but are correlated with one another because both vary according to the religiosity of the individual.

Researchers typically measure variables at one point in time. That is, data from each research participant is gathered just once. This is referred to as a *cross-sectional* research design. In contrast, sometimes researchers gather data from the same individuals at two or more points in time. Such *longitudinal* research allows researchers to gauge whether, for each individual, there are changes in certain variables over time or whether a particular variable or manipulation at one point has an effect on another variable at a later point. Cross-sectional and longitudinal research are each best suited to different types of research questions (Kaplan, 1989).

Suppose researchers hypothesize that rates of sexual activity decline with the length of time individuals are married. Because the researchers cannot randomly assign research participants to marriages of various lengths, by necessity the research will be correlational. However, the researchers have a choice between cross-sectional or longitudinal measurement of sexual activity. A cross-sectional design involves first measuring rates of sexual activity within marriages of varying duration, then correlating the length of time the couple has been married with how frequently they engage in sexual activity. If there is a negative correlation, the researchers would conclude that those who had been married longest reported the least frequent sexual activity (or conversely, those married most recently reported the most frequent sexual activity).

In this case the researchers do not know whether some aspect of being married longer *causes* declines in sexual activity. The reason is that the research participants who have been married longest are also among the oldest respondents. So, the fact that they, as a group, report less frequent sexual activity compared to the younger respondents may be due to having been members of an earlier generation, raised in a time of different cultural values (this is referred to as a *cohort effect*; Turner, Danella, & Rogers, 1995). The researchers are left wondering whether these same individuals have always had a relatively lower rate of sexual activity or whether the rate of sexual activity declined as their marriage endured (which is the researchers' hypothesis).

A longitudinal design would allow the researchers to more adequately test their hypothesis. In such a study, the same individuals would be followed over time to see if rates of sexual activity systematically change. Of course, if there are declines, the researchers are still left with the question of why or what is behind such changes, but at least there would be documentation that such declines occur (at least within that sample; see Chapter 3). If researchers using a cross-sectional design proclaim that sexual activity declines with length of marriage, skepticism should dominate over the implication that sexual activity becomes less frequent over time within individual marriages.

In conclusion, solid research starts with a solid research question, one that can be addressed adequately with the methods the researchers choose or have at their disposal. Issues of research methodology will be considered throughout much of this book. However, one should always keep in mind that, "A foolish question begets a foolish answer, regardless of whether it is asked during an in-depth interview or as part of a mailed questionnaire" (Sprey, 1995, p. 872).

In conclusion, the questions to take away from this chapter are

- *Was the research design adequate or appropriate for the research question?*
- *Was the design descriptive, experimental, quasi-experimental, or correlational?*
- *Was the design cross-sectional or longitudinal?*

WHAT KIND OF PERSON WOULD PARTICIPATE IN A STUDY LIKE THIS?

Sexuality research relies on people agreeing to participate, which typically involves sharing sensitive information about themselves, their experiences, attitudes, and reactions, with total strangers. Such participation, even if completely anonymous, still requires time and energy. Who are the people willing to give their time and energy to reveal potentially sensitive information about themselves? What is their motivation for doing so? These are important questions to ask when assessing the *generalizability* of the research findings.

GENERALIZABILITY

Researchers start with a *population* of interest, whether it be all people or adolescent boys or African American lesbian women. Because it is typically impossible, or at least not feasible, to study every member of the population of interest, researchers must rely on studying a selected group, or *sample*, of those individuals. Results are generalizable to the extent that the findings of the study (which are based on the sample) mirror what one would find in the larger population of interest. Ideally, a research sample would be perfectly *representative* of the population of interest (that is, all members of the population would have an equal chance of being included in the research). In reality, this is impossible to achieve, as there are always some potential participants who refuse the invitation to take part in the research. This is just one of the things researchers must contend with, regardless of their field of study.

The larger concern is the extent to which a particular sample deviates from the population of interest (Kaplan, 1989). If the people in the sample differ in important ways from the larger population from which they were drawn, we should question the extent to which the findings apply to the people in the population who were not part of the research sample. In such a case, we might refer to the sample as *biased*, in the sense that it is not truly representative. That is not to say that the individuals in the sample are biased toward the topic

15

being studied, but rather that the sample as a whole is biased to include more of a particular type of person than exists in the population.

Obtaining representative or unbiased samples may be especially problematic when the population of interest is small or difficult to access. For example, members of ethnic minority groups are often underrepresented in sexuality research (Wiederman, Maynard, & Fretz, 1996), as are children and elderly adults. If the population of interest is a stigmatized group, researchers often must be creative in gaining access to a sample from that stigmatized group. In these cases frequently the goal is to obtain a large enough sample to warrant analysis, rather than a representative sample per se. For example, how might researchers go about locating a large sample of gay men or lesbian women, or adults who have had sexual contact with children, or individuals who become sexually aroused by wearing rubber garments? Researchers might locate a social club, advocacy group, or Internet site frequented by members of the population of interest. However, certainly not everyone in the population of interest participates in such groups, leaving the question of how those individuals who do might differ in important ways from members of the population of interest who do not.

Ultimately, to whom are researchers intending to generalize? The answer varies from study to study, yet there are some common assumptions. For example, it is typically assumed that there are probably cross-cultural differences in many aspects of sexuality (Caron, 1998; Hatfield & Rapson, 1996). So, when researchers employ a sample of respondents from the United States and write, "Based on the findings, it appears that men are more likely than women to stimulate their own genitals for pleasure," the assumption is that we are talking about men and women in the United States. Still, even the extent to which researchers can generalize to the population of interest rests on the degree of potential *volunteer bias*.

VOLUNTEER BIAS

Research results are often presented in such a way as to imply that they accurately describe people in general, or at least all people in the population of interest. However, not everyone from the population of interest is given the opportunity to participate in research and not everyone who is given the opportunity actually agrees to do so. Because people are free to decline an invitation to participate in research, some people will choose that option, perhaps because they do not have the time or interest to participate. This is true about research in general, but we can imagine how the issue may be most relevant when the research is on a sensitive topic, such as sexuality. So, perhaps it is not surprising that even in the most extensive and well-conducted national sexuality surveys, where great care is taken to select a nationally representative sample, only about 70–80% of those people initially selected to participate actually do so (Seidman & Rieder, 1994).

Are there differences between those individuals who agree to participate in sexuality and research and those who do not? In general, volunteers for sexuality research may be more likely to be male, relatively young, more sexually experienced, more comfortable with sexual topics, and more liberal in their sexual attitudes compared to nonvolunteers (Wiederman, 1999b). So, when researchers investigate people's sexual attitudes and experiences, they may be examining a group who are different from the general population.

In addition to these differences between volunteers and nonvolunteers, the more sensitive or revealing the information requested, or the more sexually explicit the requirements of participation, the more likely the sample may deviate from the general public (Plaud, Gaither, Hegstad, Rowan, & Devitt, 1999; Wiederman, 1999b). For example, if asked to complete a brief, anonymous survey on their attitudes toward premarital sex, a small proportion of potential respondents will refuse. If the same sample of potential participants is asked to complete a face-to-face interview regarding their sexual experiences, a larger proportion of people will refuse. If the same group is asked to view sexually explicit videos while their genital responses are recorded using special instruments, an even greater proportion of people will refuse. The more sensitive or involved the research, the more questionable the generalizability of the results.

COLLEGE STUDENT PARTICIPANTS

It is important to note that a large proportion of published research reports on human sexuality are based on college student participants (Wiederman, 1999a). Students are often a captive audience, are familiar with completing surveys, and may be most open to answering questions of a sexual nature. In addition, researchers often have a difficult time securing governmental or other funding to conduct research on many topics in sexuality, leaving them to employ whatever samples are readily available (often called "convenience samples"). As noted in Chapter 1, most sexuality researchers are university faculty members, so it stands to reason that they would turn to students as research participants.

One may question how representative college students are of the general population. Many college students are only 18–22 years old, which limits the range of relationship and sexual experience they are likely to have had compared to older adults. Perhaps even more troubling is the possibility that samples of college students employed in sexuality research differ even from those college students who do not volunteer for such research. A common method of recruiting potential college student participants involves the use of a *subject pool*, which is populated with students from college courses that require participation in research to pass the course or that offer extra credit for research participation (Wiederman, 1999a). These subject pools often are part of introductory social science courses, such as Introduction to Psychology. How does the use of such subject pools result in a potentially biased sample of college students?

Courses such as Introduction to Psychology may attract certain types of college students and not others (so not all college students at a particular campus have a chance to participate in the research). Also, many times the sign-up procedures involved in recruiting individual participants from the pool include at least a brief description of the study and what participation entails. The rationale for such descriptions is that students have a right to know what to expect when they are selecting studies in which to potentially participate (the principle of *informed consent*). The problem is that such descriptions attract certain students and repel others, leading to a unique sample of college students (Wiederman, 1999a).

Perhaps you were once a student in a course requiring research participation, such as Introduction to Psychology. If so, do you remember the recruitment procedures? How did you select the studies in which you would eventually participate? If you had some knowledge of the content of those studies beforehand, do you remember being interested more in some than in others? What made for an attractive or interesting study? Perhaps it sounded stimulating or easy. Perhaps other studies seemed unappealing because of the subject matter or the tasks that were being asked of participants (too boring or too difficult). Either way, you were attracted to certain studies that some other students probably found unappealing, and vice versa. What might have distinguished you from these other students? You may have differed with regard to certain personality traits, experiences, or expectations. In any case, the samples the researchers used were not representative of even those college students taking that course that semester.

Does the representativeness of the sample really make that much difference to the result? Like so many questions in life, the answer is "it depends." Some people have argued that if a researcher's hypothesis is that two particular variables are related among people in general, then it really does not matter that one is testing the hypothesis with a biased sample, because the relationship should still exist (Brecher & Brecher, 1986). It is possible, however, that the relationships exist for some groups of people and not others, or that the strength of the relationship between the variables varies across groups.

The representativeness of the sample is most important when the research is conducted to determine the frequency or prevalence of an experience or attitude (i.e., when the study is descriptive in nature). In this case, the ways in which people who volunteer for sexuality research differ from nonvolunteers will most likely lead to distorted estimates, because volunteers have been found to report greater sexual experience and more liberal attitudes toward sexuality compared to nonvolunteers (Plaud et al., 1999; Wiederman, 1999b).

As an example, consider an extreme hypothetical case. Suppose researchers were interested in assessing the prevalence of masturbation among college students and were naive about the issues discussed in this chapter. The researchers may decide to run the following advertisement in the school newspaper: "Volunteers wanted for a study on masturbation among college students. Seeking individuals with all levels of experience. Call 555-1234." Who is likely to call? Students who have never masturbated and consider the act reprehensible? Probably not. The researchers are liable to end up with the students who are most liberal in their attitudes and most comfortable with sexuality. Even so, why would these students call? What incentive is there to take time out of their schedule to do a favor for the researchers, who, after all, are strangers?

What if the researcher offered $20 for participating in the study? This would probably help to ensure a somewhat more diverse sample, although the students most in need of cash are those who have an additional incentive. With any type of recruitment, there is always the issue of incentive. In the case of subject pools, for example, the incentive is to earn the necessary research credit to pass the course or receive extra credit. Is this enough of an incentive to take seriously one's role as a research participant, especially if participation involves tasks that are difficult or revealing information that might be embarrassing? Typically, students earn their credit by showing up and appearing to comply with requests; there is no loss of credit for answering questions hastily or inaccurately. As the demands placed on the participant increase, the researcher should be increasingly wary that participants are invested in providing accurate data.

In conclusion, the issue of generalizability is important and one that ultimately needs to be addressed empirically. Additional research that is focused on the same or similar topics helps to reveal whether the results of a study generalize well. If several researchers, each using at least slightly different methods and samples, find generally the same thing, one can conclude with greater confidence that the results of any one of those studies generalizes to the larger population of interest. Findings of sexuality research based on college student participants may or may not generalize to the national population, but only additional research with a variety of different types of samples will help answer that question.

In closing, the questions to take away from this chapter are

- *Who were the participants?*
- *How were they recruited and what incentive was there for participation?*
- *To what degree was the sample liable to be biased or the results generalizable?*

How Do Researchers Pose Sexuality Questions to Respondents?

Due to the sensitive nature of information regarding sexual experiences and attitudes, researchers must typically rely on self-reports from research participants. Although researchers can measure directly the physiological arousal or response associated with sexual stimuli (Harris & Rice, 1996; Rowland, 1999), such laboratory research is relatively rare and only applies to certain research questions (e.g., factors related to sexual dysfunction or sexual response to deviant images). So, in descriptive, experimental, and correlational studies, sexuality researchers typically ask research participants to report (in one form or another) their attitudes, reactions, or behavior.

When researchers ask people about their sexuality, either through interviews or questionnaires, there are several factors that can influence responses. Of course, one of those factors is the respondent's actual sexual attitudes or experiences (whichever one is being asked about), and ideally this would be the only factor affecting responses. If this were the case, researchers could rest assured that people's responses to their questions reflect those respondents' actual attitudes or behavior. Unfortunately, researchers have documented that participants' responses are affected by several other factors, besides their attitudes or experiences, and these other factors have been lumped together under the terms *response bias* or *reporting bias* (Catania, 1999; Catania et al., 1993; Weinhardt, Forsyth, Carey, Jaworski, & Durant, 1998).

THE RESPONDENT AND FORMS OF RESPONSE BIAS

Although the forms of response bias are numerous, I will address the few most troublesome ones and the ones that should be considered when examining any example of sexuality research. First under consideration are the primary reasons research participants may not provide perfectly accurate answers to researchers' questions, even when they try.

20

Memory and Recall

Suppose researchers presented the following question to respondents: "With how many different partners have you had vaginal intercourse during your lifetime?" Who would most likely be able to provide an accurate response? Probably those respondents who have never had vaginal intercourse, or who have had one, two, or three partners, would easily be able to recall the exact number of partners.

Now consider a respondent who in actuality has experienced vaginal intercourse with 16 partners over a span of 30 years. Some of these partners were long-term relationship partners and some were casual sexual affairs, or "one-night stands." Imagine that this respondent first had vaginal intercourse at the age of 17 and is now 47 years old (a sexual history spanning 30 years). Suppose that this person has been married since age 29 and has not had sexual intercourse with anyone outside of marriage. So, this person accumulated 15 of the total 16 partners between the ages of 17 and 29, a period that ended 18 years ago! How likely is it that, when confronted with the research question posed above, this individual will be able to recall exactly 16 partners, especially when the respondent will probably only spend a second or two arriving at an answer?

Consider a second type of example: "How many times during the past 12 months have you used your mouth to stimulate a partner's genitals?" These questions may seem strange taken out of the context of a larger questionnaire on sexual history, but they mirror closely the kinds of questions researchers ask participants. Someone who had not performed oral sex during the past year or so would easily produce an accurate response. However, what about respondents who have had several recent partners or who have had only one partner with whom they have had an ongoing sexual relationship over the previous year? Certainly it is unrealistic to expect that these respondents could remember each instance of oral sex, even if highly motivated and given enough time to try.

How do respondents produce answers to these types of questions about their behavior when it is impossible to recall and count every actual instance of the behavior? In the end, most respondents *estimate* their experience, and respondents do so in different ways depending on the frequency and regularity of the behavior about which they are being asked (Brown, 1995, 1997; Conrad, Brown, & Cashman, 1998; Croyle & Loftus, 1993). For example, in response to the number of sex partners question, respondents with several partners are liable to give an estimate (Brown & Sinclair, 1999; Wiederman, 1997b). Indeed, respondents with more than about 10 partners typically provide numbers that are multiples of 5 (e.g., 10, 15, 25, 30, 50, 75, 100). Researchers who compute the average number of reported partners and compare groups (e.g., men compared to women) will end up with decimal averages that look precise (e.g., 4.13 versus 2.27) yet are based on a substantial proportion of respondents who provided global estimates (Wadsworth, Johnson, Wellings, & Field, 1996).

Considering responses to frequency questions such as the oral sex question posed above, it appears that people who have had numerous such experiences go through a reasoning process to arrive at an estimate (Brown, 1995, 1997; Conrad et al., 1998; Jaccard & Wan, 1995). The thinking of one hypothetical respondent might go something like this, "Well, my partner and I typically have sex about twice a week or so, and I perform oral sex about half of those times. There are 52 weeks in a year, so I guess I performed oral sex about 50 times during the previous 12 months." The entire line of thinking may only take a second or two. Notice that the respondent does not even attempt to remember each instance because doing so is impossible. How accurate the resulting estimate is depends on how regularly the respondent engages in the behavior as well as the accuracy of his or her recall or estimation of that typical frequency (Downey, Ryan, Roffman, & Kulich, 1995). Minor exceptions, such as when the respondent was on vacation or was ill or was fighting with the partner, are typically not factored in when arriving at global estimates.

Degree of Insight

Taking into account the recall problems inherent in asking people to report accurately on their own behavior, consider the following sexuality questions and how accurate the responses might be:

1. What proportion of your sexual contacts have you used a condom?
2. How did you feel during your first experience of sexual intercourse?
3. What proportion of sexual interactions with your current partner have you initiated?
4. How comfortable are you communicating your desires to a sexual partner?
5. How easy is it for you to achieve orgasm during sexual activity with a partner?
6. At what age did you first stimulate your own genitals for pleasure?

Each of the questions in this list are heavily dependent on the respondent's memory, yet they also vary with regard to the degree of insight the respondent needs to have into his or her own mental processes. For example, the second and fourth questions require insight into one's emotions, whereas the first and last questions do not. Conceivably, people who are generally less introspective (less aware of their own feelings and thoughts) will probably have greater difficulty answering the second and fourth questions, and they may be more prone to providing inaccurate answers as a result.

Now consider questions that require an even greater degree of introspection:

1. Why did you decide to have sex with your current partner that first time that you did?
2. Why did you fall in love with your most recent partner?
3. Why did you break up with your most recent partner?

These questions not only demand recall but also a great degree of insight into one's own motives and the factors that led to particular emotions and decisions. Humans may not have good insight into these mental processes (Brehmer & Brehmer, 1988; Nisbett & Ross, 1980; Nisbett & Wilson, 1977), and this may be especially true with complex feelings and decisions like those involved in the three questions asked above.

When asked questions about their motives or decisions, people do readily provide responses. Here are typical answers people might give to the three questions posed above. "I felt pressured." "He was the kindest person I had ever met." "We were no longer communicating and just grew apart." Yet how well do these answers capture all of the complexity that went into deciding to engage in sexual activity for the first time, or falling in love, or ending a meaningful relationship? It may be that people provide such answers based on stereotypes or beliefs they hold regarding the causes of relationship events (Baldwin, 1992, 1995; Wilson & Stone, 1985). These stereotypes or beliefs may or may not accurately reflect what occurred within the respondent's own life.

Motivation and Social Desirability

Discussion up to this point has been centered upon problems in accuracy of recall and degree of insight that occur because of the limitations of the human brain, even when motivation and honesty are high. There are also forms of response bias that arise from low motivation to produce accurate responses, or motivation to present oneself in a certain light, regardless of the accuracy of that portrayal.

Considering lack of motivation, it is fair to ask, "How motivated are respondents when called randomly on the telephone to participate in a brief (or not so brief) telephone interview?" Or, how motivated are respondents who are participating because of the requirements of a college course they are taking? In contrast, might motivation be higher if participants are paid a substantial amount of money for participating, or if they are participating so that they will have access to clinical services (e.g., part of a screening process to qualify for a sex therapy study)?

There are no definite answers to these questions, but it is important to question the extent to which participant motivation might affect responses. Also, respondent motivation is liable to vary across participants within any given study (Groves, Cialdini, & Couper, 1992). Recall from Chapter 3 that volunteers for sexuality studies may be generally more outgoing and open about sexuality compared to people who refuse to participate (Wiederman, 1999b), and even among volunteers, some individuals may be more open and invested in the process than are others (Catania, 1999). There also may be differences between those who do not answer some questions in a sexuality survey and those who answer all questions (Kupek, 1998). For example, those individuals who omit answers to some sexuality questions have been found to be older, more conservative, and less sexually experienced compared to people who answer all the items in a sexuality questionnaire (Wiederman, 1993).

In addition, some respondents in sexuality studies may distort their responses, consciously or unconsciously, to present themselves in a positive light (Siegel, Aten, & Roughman, 1998; Tourangeau, Smith, & Rasinski, 1997). For example, if a respondent who has had several sexual partners believes that greater sexual experience is something to be proud of, she or he may tend to overestimate the lifetime number of sex partners. Conversely, if a respondent feels ashamed of something sexual from his or her past, the respondent may not remember or admit this experience in an interview or on a questionnaire. Researchers refer to these types of distortion as *social desirability response bias*, and such bias may even function as a result of the interviewer being the same or different gender as the respondent (Catania, 1999; Huygens, Kajura, Seeley, & Barton, 1996). The degree to which respondents believe their answers are anonymous can also alter the degree to which responses are tainted by social desirability response bias.

Besides conscious distortion or deceit in people's sexual self-reports, there are unconscious forms of response bias. In a fascinating example, Baldwin and Holmes (1987) randomly assigned college women to two conditions, each involving visualization of the faces of two people known to the participant. In one condition the women were asked to picture the faces of two acquaintances on campus, whereas in the other condition participants were asked to visualize the faces of two older members of their families. All of the women were subsequently presented with the same sexual story and asked to rate their responses to it. Interestingly, those women who had been asked to visualize family members rated the sexual stories less positively than did the women in the other condition. Why? It is likely that the internal "presence" of the family members led the women to respond more in line with what would be expected by the family members. In a sense, the women's responses were distorted (perhaps unconsciously) by what they had focused on prior to providing their ratings.

In summary, there are several reasons why the responses research participants give to questions about their sexuality may be inaccurate. These include constraints on memory, inaccessibility to one's own motives or other mental processes, degree of motivation, and tendencies to distort (consciously or unconsciously) one's responses to be consistent with an image of the self that one wishes to portray. So, research in which respondents have an incentive to participate, are asked questions about their behavior over short periods of time, and are assured of anonymity should produce more credible results than research in which participants have little incentive, are asked questions about their behavior over long periods of time, are asked questions about their feelings or motivations, and are unsure of their anonymity. The forms of response bias that have been focused on thus far involve factors related to the respondent. There are, however, aspects of the research itself that may result in response bias.

THE RESEARCH METHODOLOGY AND FORMS OF RESPONSE BIAS

Question Wording and Terminology

To elicit respondents' self-reports, researchers must rely on words, either spoken or printed, to form the questions (Binson & Catania, 1998; Catania et al., 1996). The problem is that any time words are used there is the possibility for misunderstanding. Can the researcher be sure that the words used in an interview or questionnaire have the same meaning to all respondents as they do to the researcher? Researchers often take great care in choosing the wording for questions, sometimes trying them out on a small sample to work out any problems before actually conducting the study (often referred to as "piloting the questions" or conducting a "pilot study"). For example, would respondents know the meaning of formal sexual terminology such as *fellatio* and *cunnilingus*? Despite care in question wording, it is easy for different meanings to arise (Huygens et al., 1996). Consider the following questions:

> How many sex partners have you had during your lifetime?
> How often have you and your partner engaged in sex during the past month?
> Have you ever forced someone to have sex against their will? (Or, have you ever been forced to have sex against your will?)
> How often do you experience sexual desire?
> How frequently do you masturbate?

Chances are that if confronted with these questions in a survey, you would generate answers quite readily, especially if a scale was provided for you to indicate frequency. However, other respondents may interpret the meaning of certain words differently than you do. In the first three questions, what does the term *sex* mean? If you are heterosexual, you are liable to interpret *sex* to mean vaginal intercourse. To many heterosexual individuals, if there was not a penis moving around inside a vagina, there was no sex. However, others will interpret "sex" to include oral or manual stimulation of the genitals (Sanders & Reinisch, 1999). How does anal intercourse figure in to the equation?

What about lesbian women (Rothblum, 1994)? Heterosexual definitions of sex rely on the involvement of a penis, and episodes of sex typically are marked by ejaculation from that penis. So, if heterosexual couples are asked the second question ("How often have you and your partner engaged in sex during the past month?"), responses will likely be based on the number of times the man in each couple ejaculated after having been inside his partner's vagina, regardless of the number of orgasms each woman did or did not have. How might lesbian respondents arrive at an answer to the same question? Would the question even have meaning for such respondents?

In the above list of questions, how might the terms *partners, forced, sexual desire*, and *masturbate* be interpreted by different respondents with different histories, different upbringing, different religious values, and so forth? Does *partners* include every individual with whom one has had any sexual contact, or only those individuals with whom one also shared an emotional relationship? How strong does the experience of sexual desire have to be to count? What about a fleeting sexual thought or fantasy? What qualifies as *force* in a sexual situation?

This last question may elicit images of physical restraint and forcing one's body on an uninterested partner, and certainly most respondents would include such experiences in their definition of forced sex. Generally, these are the kinds of experiences that researchers are interested in when studying rape. However, because many respondents may not have had such an experience, some may tend to take a more liberal definition of *forced*. Ross and Allgeier (1996) had college men individually complete a questionnaire containing several commonly used questions having to do with forcing or coercing women into having sex. Afterward, each respondent was individually interviewed to find out how he had interpreted the meaning of the words used in some of the questions. Interestingly, there were a variety of ways the college men interpreted what was meant by each question, and some of the interpretations of the questions had nothing to do with physical force. Similar variation in the way respondents interpret response choices to questions has been found; so two respondents giving the same answer may mean different things (see Cecil & Zimet, 1998; Wright, Gaskell, & O'Muircheartaigh, 1997).

The last question in the list above had do to with masturbation. I intentionally chose this term to demonstrate that some sexual words elicit a stronger emotional reaction than others. Imagine being confronted with the question "How frequently do you masturbate?" versus "How frequently do you stimulate your own genitals for sexual pleasure or release?" Is the second question less threatening and easier to answer? What if the question had been preceded with a statement about masturbation being a common experience? Referring to a particular behavior (e.g., masturbation) as relatively common may lead respondents to be more likely to admit having performed the behavior themselves (Catania et al., 1996; Raghubir & Menon, 1996). When examining the results of a sexuality study, it is important to be sensitive to the questions and terminology that were presented to respondents, because these are liable to have a substantial effect on the answers the researcher received (and is reporting to us).

Response Choices

Earlier in this chapter the point was brought up about how people are unlikely to recall every instance of their sexual behavior. If asked how frequently respondents engage in some form of sexual expression, those who have had the experience are liable to provide a quick estimate. If researchers provide response choices for such a question, for example, once per week up to more than five times per week, participants may use those response choices to generate their estimate or to determine what is "normal" (Schwartz, 1999). Perhaps most respondents feel as though they are "average" with regard to sexual experience. If so, they may tend to use the middle response choice on the assumption that the researchers know something about how frequently the experience occurs and designed the response choices so that a middle response represents the average. So, this hypothetical respondent might choose "three times per month" in one questionnaire because that is the middle response, yet if the respondents had been given another questionnaire containing the same question, he or she might have chosen "five times per month" because that is the middle response choice in the second questionnaire.

A Rose by Any Other Name

The discussion up to this point has been centered on direct questions about sexual experience. However, because researchers frequently are interested in measuring respondents' sexual attitudes, hundreds of such measures have been developed and published (Davis, Yarber, Bauserman, Schreer, & Davis, 1998). That is not to say that all of these measures are sound or actually measure what they are believed to measure. When a researcher purports to measure respondents' sexual esteem, or sexual sensation seeking, or sexual risk taking, it is important to ask what questions or survey items were used to capture this variable. Labeling a scale as measuring a particular variable does not make it so. Consider the following hypothetical scale comprised of five items:

1. I believe that I am a good sexual partner.
2. I am comfortable with my sexual thoughts and feelings.

3. There is nothing I would change about myself sexually.
4. I have been satisfied with the sexual aspects of my life.
5. I am confident of myself in sexual interactions with a partner.

Suppose that respondents are provided with a seven-point scale to indicate their degree of agreement or disagreement with each of the statements, and an overall score is generated by summing their ratings. What might this instrument measure? One researcher might conceive of this scale as measuring *sexual esteem* because the items seem to have to do with how one views oneself as a sexual partner. Another researcher might consider it a measure of *sexual comfort and satisfaction* because the items seem to have to do with being comfortable and satisfied with oneself sexually. Yet a third researcher might see it as a measure of *sexual confidence* because the items seem to involve feeling confident in oneself as a sexual partner. These three concepts, or variables, are likely to be related, and it may seem like the differences among them are trivial. However, the label chosen is liable to influence how the results are viewed and reported. For example, suppose that you encounter the following three research results from three different researchers using this particular scale. Because each thought of the scale slightly differently, the results, although consistent, might lead readers to somewhat different conclusions, especially if they did not know anything about the scale.

1. Men scored higher than did women on a measure of sexual esteem.
2. Women indicated less sexual comfort and satisfaction compared to men.
3. Compared to women, men were more sexually confident.

The process researchers use to gather evidence that a certain scale measures a particular theoretical construct is beyond the scope of this book (see Wiederman & Whitley, in press). However, the principle to take away is that it is important to consider how the theoretical variables, such as attitudes, are actually measured.

Context Effects

When people respond to questions in a questionnaire or interview, they do not respond to each question in a vacuum. That is, respondents consider the questions that came before and after a particular question when trying to determine what the researchers mean by the question (Schwartz, 1999). The impact of certain questions on other questions in the same study is referred to as *context effects*. For example, if respondents are asked to rate their degree of satisfaction with their relationships, and that question was preceded by a series of questions about sexual relationships they had experienced, respondents are liable to interpret the satisfaction question as referring to their *sexual rela-*

tionships. In contrast, if the same satisfaction question had been preceded by a series of items having to do with family relationships, respondents might be more likely to assume that the satisfaction question had to do with familial relations.

Context effects can also influence how people evaluate their attitudes or feelings. Because respondents typically provide the first appropriate answer that comes to mind (Ottati, 1997), previous questionnaire or interview items may influence responses to a current question because those previous items called to mind particular experiences, attitudes, or feelings. As a concrete example, suppose that researchers ask respondents to rate their overall satisfaction with life. If this item is preceded by several items having to do with the quality of the respondent's sexual functioning and relationships, how the respondent feels about his or her sexuality is then more likely to color how he or she rates the overall satisfaction with life (Marsh & Yeung, 1999).

Conditions and Procedures

Apart from the questions asked, the scales used, and the context in which those items are embedded, researchers may affect respondents' answers by the conditions under which they ask participants to respond (Catania, 1999; Kaplan, 1989). Imagine for a moment answering questions about your first sexual experiences, both alone and with a partner. Under what circumstances would you feel most comfortable and free to do so? Chances are you imagined writing about such experiences, not expecting anyone else to see your answers.

Indeed, as a general rule, people are more comfortable and more willing to admit personal, potentially embarrassing information about their sexuality when they are completing an anonymous questionnaire compared to when they believe others have access to their answers. So, all else being equal, one might expect people to be more likely to admit masturbation or extramarital sex when completing an anonymous questionnaire compared to answering the same questions posed in a one-to-one interview. Accordingly, people may be more likely to provide sensitive sexual information when interviewed by a computer program compared to a human interviewer (Gribble, Miller, Rogers, & Turner, 1999; Turner et al., 1998). Asking sensitive questions in front of family members or a group of peers would likely result in even lower rates of admitting particular sexual experiences compared to a stranger.

When evaluating research, it is important to ask, "Under what conditions were respondents asked to disclose personal information?" The important factor that may result in excessive bias is whether the respondents *believed* that others might see or hear their answers, not necessarily whether others actually could.

In conclusion, the questions to take away from this chapter are

- *What were the questions or measures used in the research?*
- *How motivated were respondents to provide accurate data?*
- *Did the questions ask for information the respondents were reluctant or unable to provide accurately?*
- *What scales were used and what might these scales actually measure?*
- *How might the wording of questions or the conditions under which data were gathered have influenced responses?*

WHAT DO THE RESEARCH RESULTS MEAN?

Up to this point we have considered aspects of the research that may influence the results. For example, how might the methods of participant recruitment and questioning have affected the answers (data) the research generated? This chapter examines the issue of what the results or findings actually mean. How should the findings be interpreted?

STATISTICAL SIGNIFICANCE

Researchers generally consider their findings noteworthy only if they are *statistically significant*. To someone outside of the social sciences this term might imply that the results are sizeable or substantial; after all, in common language the word *significant* is synonymous with *important*. However, the term as used in science is purely a statistical one that may have little to do with the size or importance of the relationships found among variables (Deal & Anderson, 1995). For this reason it is important to understand what researchers mean when they report that they found a statistically significant difference between groups or a statistically significant relationship between variables.

At the heart of understanding statistical significance is the notion of *samples*. Recall from Chapter 3 that researchers are nearly always studying samples rather than entire populations. For this reason, there is always the possibility that the particular sample drawn for a given study is unusual simply through random chance. To take a concrete example, imagine that someone gives you two bags made of black cloth. Inside of each bag are 100 marbles that are either red or green. Your task is to determine whether the color of the marbles in each bag is different (whether the two groups of marbles differ in proportion). However, you are not allowed to examine the population (all 200 marbles), but only a sample of 10 marbles from each bag. Now suppose that half of the marbles in each bag are green and the other half are red. As you blindly reach in and draw 10 marbles from each bag, chances are that you will get approximately equal numbers of red and green marbles. However, there is the possibility that, simply due to chance, you will draw out 9 or 10 red (or green) marbles from one of the bags. In this case, it would be easy (and logical) to conclude that the proportion of red and green marbles in each bag differs. However, the conclusion would be inaccurate because in reality the two groups of marbles do not differ. Only if you could examine both bags thoroughly would you know for sure whether the bags differ in the proportion of red and green marbles.

What do researchers do when faced with this uncertainty that comes along with studying samples rather than populations? They calculate the likelihood that the difference they found is due to chance, and if that likelihood is relatively low (usually 5% or less) then they trust, at least initially, that the difference they found reflects an actual difference in the population. Put another way, if a finding is statistically significant, there is at least a 95% chance that the finding is "real" and is not simply a result of reaching into a population and pulling out (by chance) a sample of individuals who were not typical of the population from which they came. That concept can be difficult to grasp, and you may need to read this entire section carefully several times to fully understand it. The important thing is not to become discouraged and give up. It helps to talk through the concepts with others, such as classmates or your instructor.

Note that even when a finding is statistically significant, there is still the possibility (up to a 5% chance) that the finding was simply due to chance. So, when researchers set the statistical significance level at 5%, then, on average, for every 20 studies (or 20 statistical tests within a particular study) at least one relationship or difference will be statistically significant, yet still simply due to chance. Unfortunately there is no way to tell which relationships or differences are due to chance without drawing other independent samples to check the consistency of the relationships or differences. Performing the same experiment or analyses in different samples is referred to as *replication*. If the same findings are replicated across several studies, then we can have increased confidence that the findings reflect reality rather than simply a chance finding. Unfortunately, it is the novel findings, those that have not been found before, that are often considered the most interesting by readers and other researchers, and hence the ones that grab the headlines and the space in textbooks. Thus, the findings that are typically reported may be those about which researchers should be most cautious, because these findings have yet to be replicated.

If researchers are performing only one study on a particular topic, how can they increase the likelihood that their findings will be statistically significant, perhaps to the point where there is a 99.9% likelihood that they are not due to chance? Returning to the marble example for a moment, you were restricted to withdrawing a sample of 10 marbles from each bag. Remember that there were 50 red and 50 green marbles in each bag. So, drawing out only 10 marbles left the possibility that you would end up with samples that did not closely match the population of marbles in each bag. In this case, any differences you observed between each sample would unlikely be statistically significant, because there was a relatively high likelihood that the differences were simply due to chance. Now suppose that you sampled 90 marbles from each bag. This would give you a much more accurate view of the proportions of red and green marbles in each bag, so any differences you found would be less likely the result of chance. That is, if you did find a higher proportion of red marbles from one bag when you sampled 90 marbles from each, this difference has a greater likelihood of being statistically significant than if you found the same proportions of red marbles using a smaller sample. The conclusion from this example is that differences between samples are less likely to be chance differences and more likely to be statistically significant differences when researchers employ relatively large samples.

Another instance in which researchers are likely to find statistically significant differences is when the difference found is large. Notice, then, that a statistically significant finding may or may not be a large or substantial one. All we know from the term *statistically significant* is that the finding is unlikely to be due to chance alone. The size of the difference between groups, or the relationships between variables, is more a matter of practical significance.

PRACTICAL SIGNIFICANCE

Regardless of whether the relationship between two variables, or the difference between two groups, is statistically significant, there is the issue of the absolute size of that relationship or difference. Sometimes small relationships or differences are important for scientific theory (Prentice & Miller, 1992), but for people in the general public, the primary issue is whether the research findings are large enough to be of practical importance. There are a variety of statistics researchers use as indices of practical significance (see Rosenthal & Rosnow, 1991; Rosnow & Rosenthal, 1996, 1999), but calculation of those statistics is beyond the scope of this book.

The immediate concern is the degree to which particular research findings help us better understand sexuality among individuals. For example, two or more groups may show statistically significant group differences on some variable, yet those differences might be very small in absolute terms such that they have little practical meaning. Remember, statistical significance means that the differences are unlikely to be due simply to chance, but these differences can be quite small if the samples they are based on are large. Many male-female differences fit this description (Hyde, 1994). That is, when plotting the distribution of males' and females' scores on some measure of sexual attitudes, or their reported sexual experience, the average (or mean) of those values may be slightly different, yet there is mostly overlap between the two distributions.

Unfortunately, when research results are presented in a way that entails describing one group as having more sexual experience than a second group, it is easy to infer that the members of the first group typically or invariably differ from members of the second group. This may indeed have been the case. However, a statistically significant difference between the groups may have resulted from a small subset of people in the first group who reported extreme amounts of sexual experience. In this case, the *typical* member of each group may have given very similar responses to the questions researchers posed, yet the groups differ in the *average* response because of those few respondents who gave atypical reports (and hence inflated their group's average). Describing the members of the groups as being different in general would be somewhat misleading.

MISLEADING STATISTICS AND CHARACTERIZATIONS

It is possible that, regardless of the size of the difference or relationship found, the way researchers describe or visually present their findings implies greater relationships or differences than were actually found (Deal & Anderson, 1995). I am not saying that researchers intentionally attempt to deceive readers, but rather there are times when the ways research results are reported can lead to misrepresentation of the findings. Suppose you read that in a particular sample of college students men were more likely than women to agree with the statement, "If a woman gets raped, she gets what she deserves." This description portrays men as relatively callous at best and perhaps dangerous at worst.

Now, suppose that the respondents rated their degree of agreement with the statement using a seven-point scale where 1 corresponded to *Strongly Disagree*, 4 corresponded to *Neither Agree nor Disagree*, and 7 corresponded to *Strongly Agree*. This is a common method for measuring attitudes in sexuality research (and social science research in general). Further, suppose that the researcher found that the average rating for women was 1.78 and the average rating for men was 2.56. This may have been a statistically significant difference (particularly if it was based on a large sample), yet to say that men were in greater agreement with the statement is misleading, because it is clear that both men and women generally indicated disagreement with the statement. Although it may be more accurate to say that men were less likely to disagree with the statement, the findings may not be presented this way. Perhaps there is a somewhat natural tendency for people to make sense out of findings in terms of a "positive" direction (which group displayed more of something—in this case, agreement) rather than a "negative" direction (less disagreement).

Graphs are meant to simplify presentation of findings and to provide the reader with a visual means for understanding statistical relationships. Sometimes, however, graphs imply that differences are more absolute than is actually the case. For example, consider a standard bar graph with two columns or bars, one representing the average number of sexual partners reported by men and another representing the average number of sexual partners reported by women. The two bars, presented side by side, are typically meant to illustrate the difference between the two averages. The potential problem is that the bars have very definite boundaries where each stops. The variability within each group and the degree of overlap between the groups is not represented well in such graphs. So, it is easy to conclude that the typical man (or every man?) reported a greater number of sexual partners than did the typical woman. Also, the units of measurement can be manipulated in graphs to make an effect appear larger or smaller visually. It is important to examine closely the numbers associated with graphs, rather than relying on the visual impression they create.

Percentages, too, can be misleading. As an example, consider the results from analyses performed by Wortley and Fleming (1997). These researchers examined the prevalence of AIDS in men and women in the United States, particularly from the period 1991 to 1995. Based on their findings, Wortley and Fleming (1997) concluded that "the incidence of AIDS has increased more in women than men in recent years" (p. 914). If all one read was the conclusion, one might be led to believe that AIDS is more prevalent in women than in men, or quickly becoming so. Examining their data more closely, however, reveals a potential problem with percentages.

It is true that, from 1991 to 1995, new cases of AIDS among men increased about 11% compared to an increase of about 60% among women (see Wortley & Fleming, 1997, Figure 1). Even these percentages imply more of an epidemic among women than among men. However, in terms of absolute number of new cases of AIDS in 1995, there were about 50,000 cases among men compared to about 13,000 cases among women. Clearly, most cases of AIDS were still occurring among men (in 1991 it was about 45,000 new cases among men compared to about 8,000 cases among women). It was accurate to say that the percentage increase from 8,000 cases to 11,000 cases among women is larger than the percentage increase from 45,000 cases to 50,000 cases among men, but without considering the absolute number of cases, the overall conclusion regarding the percentages may mislead the reader.

Even these numbers do not tell the whole story for women. While it was true that new cases of AIDS were occurring at a faster rate among women than among men from 1991 to 1995, the incidence of AIDS was not equally distributed among women in general. A new case of AIDS in the United States in 1995 occurred among every 33,300 women of European descent, every 62,500 Asian American women, every 4,200 Latina women, and every 2,000 African American women (see Wortley & Fleming, 1997, Table 1). Obviously, to make generalizations about American women, as though they were a homogeneous group, also would lead to misrepresentation of the data.

A similar way percentages may be interpreted in a way that is confusing has to do with describing the difference between two groups in relative rather than absolute terms. The conclusion that "Members of Group A were four times more likely than members of Group B to report having been raped" implies a substantial difference between the two groups. However, the absolute percentages may have been 2% in Group A compared to .5% in Group B. Similarly, the incidence of some behavior or disease or experience may have doubled in the past year or decade. This conclusion may be based on the finding that the incidence increased from one out of every 10,000 people to two out of every 10,000 people. The increase sounds more dramatic when presented as a percentage compared to the absolute numbers. If a writer does not present the actual numbers, but rather provides only the percentages, the magnitude of the problem should remain in doubt. In addition, a number that is preceded by the phrase "as many as" most likely represents an upper limit as to estimates, and the actual number is probably lower (and may be considerably lower).

DO THE CONCLUSIONS MATCH THE RESEARCH DESIGN?

Are the conclusions the authors draw from their findings, or the ways in which they characterize their findings, legitimate given the nature of the research? In asking this question, the discussion has come full circle from considering the research design and the inherent limitations involved with each type of research (see Chapter 2). Under consideration now is whether, given those limitations, the conclusions seem warranted.

As an example, suppose researchers claim that the results of their research show that living together before marriage results in increased likelihood of divorce within five years after marriage. The researchers are basing this conclusion on the finding that a greater proportion of people who lived together prior to marriage divorced within five years when compared to respondents who had not lived together (see Cunningham & Antill, 1994, and DeMaris & Rao, 1992, for examples). Although the researchers found such a relationship, the conclusion implies that there is something about premarital cohabitation that *causes* an increased risk for divorce.

Recall, however, that correlational research does not allow us to draw conclusions about causality. In this case, there may be some other variable or set of variables that is related to both cohabitation and divorce that better explains their apparent relationship. For example, people who lived together before marriage may be less religious and hold more liberal attitudes regarding relationships, sexuality, and family compared to those couples who did not live together (Forste & Tanfer, 1996). People who are less religious and hold liberal attitudes about relationships may also be more open to the possibility of divorce when things are not going well in the marriage. These group differences in religiosity and attitudes, which existed before cohabitation, may best explain why those who chose premarital cohabitation were also more likely to divorce.

Rosenthal (1994) referred to researchers' tendencies to imply causal relationships between their variables as "causism." He noted that writers may not come out and say that their correlational results indicate a causal relationship, yet they may describe their findings using such words as *effect*, *impact*, *consequence*, or *the result of*. In using such words when describing relationships between two variables, the implication is that one variable caused the other or at least influenced it. Such words distract the reader from the important point that the results are simply correlational, and that all we can say for sure is that the two variables demonstrate a statistical relationship (and perhaps a weak, yet statistically significant, one).

If researchers do not consider possible third variables that might explain the correlation between any two variables, there is the possibility that the findings will be misleading. For example, in one study the researchers found that religiosity and engaging in risky sexual encounters were negatively correlated among college women (Poulson, Eppler, Satterwhite, Wuensch, & Bass, 1998). Those college women in the sample who were most religious were least likely to report having engaged in risky sex. However, they also found that religiosity and risky sex were related to an important third variable: alcohol consumption. It appears that religiosity and risky sex were related to each other because each of these variables were related to likelihood of drinking alcohol prior to engaging in sexual activity.

In another example, researchers reported that respondents with less than a high school education were about half as likely to report having had a sexually transmitted disease (STD) compared to respondents with at least a high school education (Tanfer, Cubbins, & Billy, 1995). If that is the only statement we encounter, it might be tempting to conclude that people with greater education are actually more likely to contract an STD. However, STD infections were self-reported, and educational level may be related to both awareness of STDs and the likelihood of having access to health care (so that an STD might be detected). It is likely that the most educated respondents in the sample were most aware of STDs and their symptoms, and most likely to seek medical care that might result in detection of any STDs that are present. Accordingly, all we can conclude from this study is that more educated respondents were more likely to *report* having had an STD.

There are numerous ways in which the limitations or flaws in a research study might be glossed over when it comes to drawing conclusions about the findings. These include making generalizations that are not warranted based on the sample. For example, researchers may survey college students about attitudes toward condoms and conclude from those results that people in general hold certain attitudes. It is also common not to recognize the limitations of the measures or questions that were presented to respondents (see Chapter 4). For example, researchers may ask respondents about their sexual experiences and draw conclusions based on the answers that imply that the respondents did indeed have such experiences. To do so does not explicitly recognize the possibility that the answers respondents provided were inaccurate due to problems with memory, difficulty understanding the intended meaning of the questions, and concerns over presenting themselves in a socially desirable light (see Chapter 4).

To return to the religiosity and risky sex study described above (Poulson et al., 1998), perhaps religiosity was not related to actual consumption of alcohol or engaging in risky sex among the college women in the sample, but rather the most religious women in the sample were most likely to distort their self-reported alcohol consumption and experience with risky sex. Similarly, to return to the education and STD study described above (Tanfer et al., 1995), perhaps respondents with the least education reported the fewest STDs not because of a reduced incidence of STDs among this group, but because of a greater tendency to distort their memory of having had STDs or a greater tendency to lie about such STDs.

In conclusion, before examining particular research topics in the remaining chapters, the questions to take away from this chapter are

- *What do the research results mean?*
- *How strong were the relationships between variables or how large were the differences between groups?*
- *Were any of the summary statistics (percentages, means, relationships) presented in a way that could be misleading?*
- *Were the conclusions warranted given the research design, participants, and measures?*

THE APPLICATIONS

One thing I have learned in a long life:
that all our science, measured against reality,
is primitive and childlike—and yet it is the
most precious thing we have.
—Albert Einstein

The only alternative to gathering information
that might be misleading is to gather no information.
That is not progress.
—David C. Funder

CORE QUESTIONS:

1. Was the research design adequate or appropriate for the research question?
   a. Was the design descriptive, experimental, quasi-experimental, or correlational?
   b. Was the design cross-sectional or longitudinal?
2. Who were the participants?
   a. How were they recruited, and what incentive was there for participation?
   b. To what degree was the sample liable to be biased or the results generalizable?
3. What were the questions or measures used in the research?
   a. How motivated were respondents to provide accurate data?
   b. Did the questions ask for information the respondents were reluctant or unable to provide accurately?
   c. What scales were used, and what might these actually measure?
   d. How might the wording of questions or the conditions under which data were gathered have influenced responses?
4. What do the research results mean?
   a. How strong were the relationships between variables, or how large were the differences between groups?
   b. Were any of the summary statistics (percentages, means, relationships) presented in a way that could be misleading?
   c. Were the conclusions warranted given the research design, participants, and measures?

Behavior: Do Males and Females Differ in Sexual Experience?

Potential male-female differences seem to be a core feature of the study of sexual attitudes and experience (Hatfield & Rapson, 1993; Schwartz & Rutter, 1998), and several such differences have been reported across studies (Oliver & Hyde, 1993). Investigating male-female differences may be appealing to researchers because the process seems straightforward: Ask respondents whether each is male or female, then compare the two groups with regard to sexual attitudes or experiences. However, interpretation of the results from such studies is not always so straightforward.

Was the Research Design Adequate or Appropriate for the Research Question?

Studies examining male-female differences are based on comparison groups formed according to respondents' answers to a question about their sex ("Are you male or female?"). Accordingly, such studies are correlational by definition. That is, researchers cannot randomly assign respondents to the groups "male" and "female," nor do they attempt to change respondents' self-ascribed sex. So, such studies clearly are not experiments (recall that an experiment requires both treatment of some form as well as random assignment to each treatment group). Researchers simply correlate self-reported sex with whatever sexuality variable is being considered.

Correlational studies always have the issue of undetermined causality. That is, if researchers find a relationship between (self-reported) biological sex and sexual experience, all the researchers can say for sure is that the two variables appear to be related in a statistical sense. Because in a correlational study researchers do not manipulate either variable, it is uncertain which variable affects the other, or whether both are due to some other third variable or set of variables. In the case of male-female differences, however, researchers often assume that, because the individual was ascribed a sex at birth, his or her

41

anatomical sex is liable to have affected sexual experience rather than the individual's sexual experience somehow affecting their biological sex. The latter possibility is implausible, as the individual's ascribed sex preceded his or her sexual experience. Perhaps this is one reason why studies on male-female differences in sexuality seem so attractive; interpretation of results appears less ambiguous (at least at first) compared to many other correlational studies.

It is important to remember that researchers studying male-female differences in sexuality are locked into a correlational design, even if the study includes an aspect that is an experiment. For example, suppose researchers hypothesize that men and women respond differently in their verbal descriptions of arousal in response to violent pornography but not in response to nonviolent pornography. In this case the researchers would randomly assign men who volunteered to participate in the study to one of two groups: exposure to violent pornography versus exposure to nonviolent pornography. The researchers would also do the same with women volunteers.

The hypothesis in this example might be that there would be gender differences in one condition but not the other. Note, however, that even though manipulation of the pornography variable entails an experimental design, the researchers are not manipulating respondent sex. So, even if the hypothesis is supported by the results, in the end the researchers found a correlation between biological sex and response in the violent pornography condition (and did not find such a correlation in the nonviolent pornography condition). If the researchers compared responses across the two experimental conditions, and there was a difference, they could conclude that type of pornography caused a difference in response. However, finding a male-female difference in either or both experimental conditions still does not warrant the conclusion that biological sex caused differences in response to the pornographic images.

Regardless of the type of research methodology, any time researchers are attempting to conclude that males and females differ with regard to some sexual experience the generalizability of the sample is a primary concern. That is, finding male-female differences in a study that mirror male-female differences that exist in the larger population depends on having a research sample in which neither the males nor the females deviate substantially from their male or female peers who did not participate in the study. So, the next question to consider is, Who is participating in the research?

WHO WERE THE PARTICIPANTS?

Because the primary research question is whether males and females differ with regard to sexual experience, any form of participant recruitment that may bias the sample toward men or women who are unusual for their gender is a major concern. For example, when potential research participants know in advance that the research focuses on sexuality, males may be more likely than females to volunteer, and this may especially be the case when the research is sexually explicit (Wiederman, 1999b). Across both males and females, volunteers for sexuality research appear to be relatively young, more sexually experienced, more comfortable with sexual topics, and more liberal in their sexual attitudes compared to nonvolunteers (Wiederman, 1999b). If any of these variables might be related to sexual experience more for one sex than the other, then the results of research on male-female differences in sexual experience might be biased as well.

The potential effects of participant recruitment can be substantial. Imagine an example in which two sets of researchers each investigate potential male-female differences in sexual experience. Perhaps the teams of researchers are collaborating and each decides to collect data at their own university for comparison across college campuses. Because the two samples will be compared, the two sets of researchers agree to use the same questionnaire. However, they do not discuss the wording of advertisements each will use to recruit respondents. So, the first group of researchers advertise for volunteers to participate in a study on "romantic relationship experience." The second group of researchers advertise for volunteers to participate in a study on "the variety and range of sexual behaviors and experiences among college students."

It is not hard to imagine that different types of people are liable to volunteer for each study (although the studies are actually the same). Further, the second group of researchers are likely to end up with a more sexually experienced sample compared to the first set of researchers. However, could the two methods of recruitment result in discrepant findings with regard to male-female differences in sexual experience? One could speculate that such would be the case. For example, respondents to the first advertisements (romantic relationship experience study) do not even know the questions have to do with sexual experience. Because college student women are less likely than their male peers to volunteer for a sexuality study, and the more sexually explicit the study the more volunteers are to be highly sexually experienced (Wiederman, 1999b), the first set of researchers might find less of a male-female difference in sexual experience compared to the second set of researchers. If the two teams never compare notes on methods of recruitment, they are liable to try to explain their discrepant findings with regard to how the two universities differ (which may indeed explain at least a part of any such discrepancy).

WHAT WERE THE QUESTIONS OR MEASURES USED IN THE RESEARCH?

The way researchers ask about respondent sex is self-explanatory and rather consistent across investigators. However, the way questions about sexual experience or behavior are worded varies widely and has important implications for the results researchers generate. The conditions under which questions are posed, and the expectations and beliefs respondents hold, also contribute to the answers researchers receive.

Potential response bias may explain some illogical findings on male-female differences in sexual experience. For example, across numerous studies conducted in various cultures and with different types of samples, males generally report greater numbers of sexual intercourse partners during their lifetime than do females (Brown & Sinclair, 1999; Wiederman, 1997b), and males are more likely than females to report using contraception (Ezeh & Mboup, 1997). Because each of these experiences (using contraception and adding a new heterosexual partner) involves both a male and a female, the average responses among males and females should be very similar. Nonetheless, discrepancies between men's and women's responses are often quite substantial. Why?

There are likely to be multiple answers to this question, and each answer probably contributes something to the total explanation (Wiederman, 1997b). In considering response bias, however, there are several specific possibilities. Perhaps males and females differ with regard to how each interprets such words as *partner, contraception,* and *intercourse.* Maybe one sex is more motivated or more able than the other to provide accurate responses. Perhaps males or females are generally more honest. There may be male-female differences in what is considered a socially desirable response. Of course, all of these explanations and more could be accurate to some degree, and when their effects combine, researchers might observe substantial male-female differences in some self-reports.

Some empirical research exists on the potential of response bias to explain male-female differences in self-reported sexual experience. For example, males may be more likely than females to include a wide range of behaviors in their definition of what constitutes "having sex" (Jeannin, Konings, Dubois-Arber, Landert, & Van Melle, 1998; Sanders & Reinisch, 1999). Compared to females, males may be more accepting of casual sex (Chara & Kuennen, 1994; Feldman, Turner, & Araujo, 1999) and may consider sexual activity a more important aspect of heterosexual relationships (Clark, Shaver, & Abrahams, 1999; Wiederman & Allgeier, 1993). In contrast, females may be more likely than males to prefer sexual activity within an emotionally intimate relationship (Geer, 1996; Sedikides, Oliver, & Campbell, 1994) and to report having a negative emotional reaction, such as guilt or regret, in response to sexual experience (Donald, Lucke, Dunne, & Raphael, 1995; Oliver & Hyde, 1993). These possible male-female differences could lead to males being more likely than females to report (or to overreport) their degree of sexual experience because they are relatively more casual and comfortable about such experience.

Another possible explanation for male-female differences in self-reported sexual experience involves possible male-female differences in memory for sexual experiences. People may tend to remember emotional events more easily than events that were unemotional (Croyle & Loftus, 1993), and females may tend to have a relatively better memory for emotional experiences compared to males (Davis, 1999). Because females are more likely than males to have an emotional reaction to sexual activity with a partner, perhaps females are generally more accurate than males in recalling sexual experiences and number of different partners (Brown & Sinclair, 1999). Some researchers have compared respondents' self-reported age at first sexual intercourse during surveys conducted at different times. This way one can gauge how consistent respondents are, and indeed females were somewhat more consistent than were males (Dunne et al., 1997; Lauritsen & Swicegood, 1997).

Females may have better memories for sexual events, but there may be other factors that help explain male-female differences in self-reports of sexual experience. For example, compared to females, males may be more likely to think and fantasize about sexual activity (Jones & Barlow, 1990; Leitenberg & Henning, 1995), seek out and expose themselves to sexually explicit media such as videos and magazines (Malamuth, 1996), and masturbate (Oliver & Hyde, 1993). During masturbation, many males may fantasize about engaging in sexual activity with a number of different partners (Ellis & Symons, 1990). Exposing themselves to sexual images, both mentally and in media, could bias a male's perceptions of actual events involving sexual activity. Such a phenomenon might explain previous research results showing that males tend to overestimate the extent to which female partners initiated sexual activity (Anderson & Aymami, 1993), underestimate the number of dates that occurred prior to sexual intercourse within their latest relationship (Cohen & Shotland, 1996), and overestimate the frequency with which they have had sexual intercourse during the recent past (Berk, Abramson, & Okami, 1995). Perhaps repeated mental and media exposure to images of sexual activity make males less able to recall accurately with how many *real* females they had sexual intercourse, particularly among those individuals who indeed have had several partners (Wiederman, 1997b).

Males and females may differ in problems with recall of sexual experience or the ways they attempt to estimate experience (Brown & Sinclair, 1999), but beliefs about gender differences themselves may also bias individuals toward reporting what they believe is expected of members of their sex. There is a large amount of research literature concerned with peoples' stereotypes regarding male-female differences (Basow, 1992), some of which have to do with beliefs about differences in male and female sexuality. For example, people may tend to believe that males have stronger sex drives than do females (Kane & Schippers, 1996) and that sexual desire is more likely to be linked to emotional intimacy for females than for males (Regan & Berscheid, 1996). Such beliefs could lead males and females to provide responses that match the stereotypes, especially when the respondents do not have a solid memory of particular sexual events or good insight into their actual motives.

In addition to unintentional distortion in responses, males and females may differ in their honesty when responding to sexual questions. Honesty is always an important issue to consider when researchers are asking people about sensitive topics such as sexuality (Lewontin, 1995; Nicholas, Durrheim, & Tredoux, 1994). Although there has been little direct research on this issue, it appears that, compared to males, females at least report being more honest in response to sexuality surveys (Wiederman, 1997b), particularly among adolescents (Siegel et al., 1998). Of course it is difficult to measure honesty, because there is no gold standard against which to compare respondents' reports of sexual experience. By asking respondents to indicate whether they were honest in their responses, researchers may prompt people to lie about their lying.

Issues of honesty and providing socially desirable responses are particularly important under certain research conditions. If questions are posed under conditions in which the respondents' anonymity or the confidentiality of responses are compromised, researchers should be skeptical of the results. For example, in one study, respondents were more likely to report having ever masturbated when they felt assured that their responses were anonymous compared to when they believed that someone might see their response while the respondent was still present (Fisher & Alexander, 1999). Interestingly, in that study the largest male-female difference in self-reported masturbation occurred when respondents believed that their responses were *not* anonymous. It may be that assuming the presence of an "audience" results in respondents providing the most socially desirable responses, and hence perhaps the largest male-female differences.

As has been shown, male-female differences in self-reported sexual experience can be the result of many factors other than actual male-female differences in such experience. Accordingly, when researchers interpret their findings on such male-female differences, they should remain cautious as to what the results actually mean.

WHAT DO THE RESEARCH RESULTS MEAN?

Depending on the research design, participants, and measures, the conclusions that can be drawn from any particular study on male-female differences in sexuality may vary considerably. Perhaps in no other area should we be more aware of the possibility that what respondents report may not accurately reflect their actual behavior and experience. So, at a very basic level, it is generally more accurate to conclude that "males and females differed in their *self-reported* experience" than it is to conclude that "males and females differed in their experience." This may seem like a picky point, yet the latter conclusion implies a definitiveness that is not warranted when the results are based on self-reports (which are vulnerable to many biasing influences).

If researchers report a male-female difference in some aspect of sexual attitudes or experience, one question to consider is, "How large is the difference?" Recall from Chapter 5 that, especially when based on a large sample, a difference between two groups (in this case males and females) can be statistically significant yet rather small in absolute terms. However, when research results are reported, often the implication is that males and females typically or invariably differ in some experience or attitude. Researchers may conclude that "males had greater numbers of sexual intercourse partners than did females" or that "males masturbated more frequently than did females." These statements imply that the typical male had more experience than did the typical female. This may indeed have been the case. However, a statistically significant difference between the groups may have resulted from a small subset of men in the sample who reported extremely large numbers of partners or extremely frequent masturbation. In these cases, the *typical* male and female in the sample may have given very similar responses to the questions researchers posed, yet the groups differ in the *average* response because of those relatively few respondents who gave atypical reports (and hence inflated the group average).

Oliver and Hyde (1993) performed a meta-analysis on the previously published research that examined male-female differences in sexual attitudes and experience. They mathematically synthesized the findings of dozens of individual studies conducted by various researchers. In the end, there were small-to-medium gender differences with regard to many of the sexuality variables. The statistics that are used to illustrate the size of the differences in the meta-analysis do not have any meaning to people who have not had some training in those statistics. However, to illustrate the typical size of those male-female differences, consider attitudes toward extramarital sex reported by samples of men compared to samples of women.

In general, men report more accepting attitudes than do women (Oliver & Hyde, 1993), yet there is substantial overlap. If there were no male-female differences, then each time a male and female were randomly selected from the population, the male would have more accepting attitudes than the female 50% of the time. Based on Oliver and Hyde's meta-analysis, men apparently have the more accepting attitudes 61% of the time. The largest gender difference Oliver and Hyde (1993) found was with regard to the incidence of masturbation. In this case, men would be more likely than women to have masturbated in 83% of cases in which a male and female are randomly selected from the population and compared. To put this in perspective, if young adult male and female individuals were randomly sampled as pairs and compared on height, men would be taller than women in 92% of cases.

We also should be sensitive to reports that tend to overgeneralize from the findings. Statements such as "males tended to have had a certain experience whereas females did not" most likely gloss over many similarities among individual males and females in the sample. This particular statement seems to imply that all males in the sample reported a particular experience, whereas none of the females did. Is this really what the researchers or journalist reporting on the research mean? With regard to generalizing beyond the sample studied, might the male-female differences vary as a function of respondent age? If researchers report finding male-female differences in sexual experience among college students, does this necessarily mean that similar male-female differences would be found among middle-aged respondents (most of whom are probably married or involved in other long-term relationships)? If there is a particular male-female difference found among older respondents, would this necessarily be the case among younger respondents (who were raised in perhaps a more liberal period of history)?

Even if male-female differences are found in a well-conducted study, there is still the question of what is behind those male-female differences. Because male-female comparisons are based on biological sex, it is easy to fall into the trap of implying or assuming that any differences found in the sexual attitudes or experience of males and females are due to some inherent biological difference. However, such male-female differences may be the result of differences between males and females with regard to some other variable, including memory, self-report tendencies, social desirability response bias, the ways individuals are raised by parents and treated by teachers and peers, cultural expectations, gender roles, and societal scripts.

Finding male-female differences in some aspect of sexuality is only the beginning of understanding. Instead of implying anything conclusive, research results indicating male-female differences should simply prompt the follow-up question, "Why do males and females appear to differ in this way?"

QUESTIONS FOR DISCUSSION

1. How might researchers go about generating a sample of males and females if the goal were to find the largest male-female differences possible with regard to sexual experience? What about if the goal were to find the smallest possible male-female differences?

2. What forms of possible male-female differences in sexual experience are illogical in that the experiences require both a male and female partner? What aspects of sexual experience do not have such a require-

ment, and therefore large male-female differences in these experiences are possible?

3. Suppose you encountered the following headline: "Research Shows That Men Want Sex More Often Than Women Do." What questions would you have if this were the only information you were given?

CASE FOR ANALYSIS

Suppose that university faculty members conduct a telephone survey of 1,000 people regarding number of sexual partners among males and females. Potential respondents are contacted as a machine randomly dials telephone numbers within the local calling area. Because the researchers employ student research assistants, all calls are conducted during the morning or afternoon, and the large majority of student assistants are female. Some people who are contacted hang up immediately or politely decline to participate upon learning the nature of the survey. In the end, 58% of those contacted provide answers to the survey questions. About two thirds of the people contacted are female, but because the males who are contacted are more likely than the females to agree to participate, the researchers end up with fairly equal numbers of male and female participants. Males report an average of 3.37 sexual partners during their lifetime, whereas females report an average of 1.65, which is a statistically significant difference. A local newspaper describes the study under the headline: "Men Have Twice as Many Sex Partners Than Women Do, Research Shows."

PUBLISHED REPORTS FOR FURTHER PRACTICE

Donald, M., Lucke, J., Dunne, M., & Raphael, B. (1995). Gender differences associated with young people's emotional reactions to sexual intercourse. *Journal of Youth and Adolescence, 24,* 453–464.

Leitenberg, H., Detzer, M. J., & Srebnik, D. (1993). Gender differences in masturbation and the relation of masturbation experience in preadolescence and/or early adolescence to sexual behavior and sexual adjustment in young adulthood. *Archives of Sexual Behavior, 22,* 87–98.

Meston, C. M., Trapnell, P. D., & Gorzalka, B. B. (1996). Ethnic and gender differences in sexual behavior between Asian and non-Asian university students. *Archives of Sexual Behavior, 25,* 33–72.

Schwartz, I. M. (1999). Sexual activity prior to coital initiation: Comparisons between males and females. *Archives of Sexual Behavior, 28,* 63–69.

Smith, A. M. A., Rosenthal, D. A., & Reichler, H. (1996). High schoolers' masturbatory practices: Their relationship to sexual intercourse and personal characteristics. *Psychological Reports, 79,* 499–509.

Sprecher, S., Barbee, A., & Schwartz, P. (1995). "Was it good for you too?" Gender differences in first sexual intercourse experiences. *The Journal of Sex Research, 32,* 3–15.

Van den Bossche, F., & Rubinson, L. (1997). Contraceptive self-efficacy in adolescents: A comparative study of male and female contraceptive practices. *Journal of Sex Education and Therapy, 22,* 23–29.

MATE SELECTION: WHAT DETERMINES PEOPLE'S CHOICE OF PARTICULAR PARTNERS?

Virtually everyone has a sexual relationship at some point, and many people have multiple sexual relationships over the course of a lifetime. Because sexual activity with a partner requires the involvement of another individual, an important question is, "What determines people's choice of partners?" Why do individuals choose certain partners and not others with whom to share romantic and sexual involvement? This seemingly simple question has generated a great deal of research, most of it focused on "mate selection criteria," or people's preferences for partners for short- or long-term relationships. This chapter examines the extent to which such research might reveal something about the process through which relationship partners select each other.

WAS THE RESEARCH DESIGN ADEQUATE OR APPROPRIATE FOR THE RESEARCH QUESTION?

The primary issue involves causality—what causes people to choose the partners they do? Of course, to determine causality, researchers would need to experimentally manipulate partner characteristics so that researchers could examine the effect of particular characteristics on respondents' reactions to potential partners. Researchers would need to have control over partner characteristics and then present potential partners to respondents for evaluation. On the surface it appears that researchers could do this by creating descriptions of potential partners, or by presenting real people, and asking research participants to indicate the degree to which each potential partner would be acceptable as a mate or sexual partner. This research design would probably represent real life more so than questionnaires that simply ask respondents why each chose their current or most recent partner. However, the experimental condition still would not mirror what occurs in real life.

In the real world, potential mates and sexual partners meet, each being at a particular point in his and her life, and feelings either do or do not emerge.

51

People's previous experiences and current situation undoubtedly influence their attraction to potential mates and the emotions that result. Also, the processes of attraction, mate selection, and sexual decision making all involve social interaction, oftentimes over multiple meetings. Similarly, mate selection is a mutual process, and people probably base some of their evaluation of potential partners on how those potential partners react to flirtation and expressed interest. These interpersonal interactions typically take place along with other activities, such as eating, drinking alcoholic beverages, being entertained, attending a party or social gathering, and so forth. The extent to which these other activities, and the moods they foster, influence mate selection decisions would not be re-created in the laboratory. So, asking respondents to imagine being interested in particular potential mates would likely not mirror the process of mate selection as it is experienced in the real world.

Despite its serious limitations, the most common research method that has been used to study mate selection processes has been the questionnaire, probably because of convenience. Such questionnaires typically contain a list of characteristics, and respondents are asked to rate how important each is in selecting a mate or sexual partner (e.g., Hatfield & Sprecher, 1995) or to rate a hypothetical partner who is described for the respondent (e.g., Desrochers, 1995; Herold & Milhausen, 1999; Wiederman & Dubois, 1998). Sometimes questionnaire studies are based on simply asking respondents to describe or list the most important influences in their mate selection experiences. There are potential problems with these types of measures, as described below. However, a primary concern with these types of studies, as discussed so far, is their potential lack of correspondence to real-life conditions. That is, respondents are asked how important each characteristic is, or to list important characteristics, in the abstract. Such characteristics are then presented or considered in relative isolation, whereas in real life, partners represent a total package of positive and negative traits, visually apparent characteristics, and reactions to us.

Another method researchers have used to examine mate selection preferences involves measuring characteristics of actual mates and then correlating those characteristics with the degree of sexual involvement, satisfaction, or partner similarity within the couple. This method represents an improvement over more direct questionnaires in that at least real couples and relationships are being studied. A primary concern, however, is that such individuals are already involved in relationships, so the extent to which currently measured traits match characteristics present at the start of interactions between the partners remains unknown. That is, by the time couples are established, each partner has probably influenced the other in many ways. So, by attempting to measure degree of similarity between partners, for example, researchers are left unsure whether the partners started out more or less similar to each other than they are now.

In summary, a primary concern with the research design used in studies of mate selection involves how well the research conditions mirror real life. A large part of that issue has to do with who the research participants are.

WHO WERE THE PARTICIPANTS?

As noted earlier, a substantial proportion of research on human sexuality is based on college student participants, and the same is true for research on mate selection and partner preferences. In some ways, college students represent an appropriate study sample, as most are in their late teens or early twenties, and most have yet to marry or select a more-or-less permanent partner. For many, being a college student entails meeting new people, dating, and selecting partners for romantic and sexual relationships. In this regard, mate selection processes are relevant to many college students.

Despite the apparently good fit between the research topic and the typical sample, there are ways in which mate selection research among college students may not generalize to other populations. For one, might there be differences between college students and people of the same age range who do not attend college? Do college student samples overrepresent particular ethnic or socioeconomic groups, such as the middle and upper classes and those of European descent? What about older adults? Do the same mate-selection preferences or processes apply when one is no longer in college, or when one has been divorced or has had other experiences with long-term relationships? How does having children, or being ready to have children, alter the picture? These are potentially important questions that studies employing college student samples are not likely to address.

With regard to generating a sample of research participants, potential biases may arise from particular recruitment strategies. Even with regard to college students, the types of courses from which participants are recruited may lead to sampling particular types of students who are not representative of all students enrolled at that particular institution. How might results differ if one team of researchers gathered data from students enrolled in sexuality courses and marriage and family courses, whereas another group of researchers recruited respondents from mathematics and engineering courses? How might answers to questions about mate selection differ among samples recruited from churches, marriage counseling centers, and meetings of the National Organization of Women? One might expect that the first group would be relatively conservative, the second group rather negative, and the third group relatively nontraditional with regard to views about mate selection and sexual relationships. The types of participants sampled can have a profound effect on research results, as can the questions posed or the measures used.

WHAT WERE THE QUESTIONS OR MEASURES USED IN THE RESEARCH?

A good deal of research on mate selection is based on self-report questionnaires, often which include lists of mate characteristics to be rated (e.g., Wiederman & Allgeier, 1992). A primary problem with such questionnaires is that respondents are assumed to have good insight into what influences their feelings and decisions (e.g., how important particular mate characteristics are in their actual experiences). An additional assumption is that partner selection is a somewhat rational process, whereby individuals cognitively evaluate potential partners and consciously choose the "best" or most appropriate one. As anyone who has experienced intense infatuation or a love affair can attest, the process from first meeting to emotional involvement can be anything but a rational, conscious one.

Another problem with presenting a list of characteristics for respondents to rate is that people are liable to provide answers that are consistent with what respondents believe should be the case. These beliefs might be based on relationship stereotypes or ideas about what "should" be (Baldwin, 1992, 1995). So, asking someone about the extent to which social status is an important characteristic in a potential mate is liable to result in fairly low ratings, because most people probably believe that to use such a criterion is shallow or unromantic. In contrast, characteristics such as *kindness, generosity*, and *patience* are liable to be rated highly. In reality, however, people who are not so kind, generous, or patient also end up with mates. Would the partners of these people have said that these qualities are unimportant? Probably not. So in some ways there are probably important differences between people's mate selection ideals and the reality of mate selection (Fletcher, Simpson, Thomas, & Giles, 1999).

What about studying actual couples? In these types of studies, many of the measures of personality or other characteristics are typically self-report in nature. So, the extent to which self-report biases are present is a concern, as is the fact that people's beliefs about romantic relationships in general affect how each perceives his or her actual relationship partner (Baldwin, 1992, 1995; Knee, 1998). Any questions or measures that rely on respondents' memories or perceptions of how things "used to be" within the relationship are vulnerable to distortion. Over time, as couples develop a history together, they construct accounts to explain (to themselves and others) how and why their relationships developed as they did (Sternberg, 1995). Then, recollection of earlier events, feelings, and perceptions within the relationship tend to be influenced by the accounts themselves (LaRossa, 1995; McGregor & Holmes, 1999). Research based on such measures leads to results that are questionable if taken at face value.

Beyond the problematic nature of self-report measures, particular research conditions may also facilitate certain forms of bias. For example, respondents might complete measures differently if they believe that their partner could see or learn of their responses, or that their responses would be compared to those of their partner. Similarly, respondents might provide different answers to questions about their romantic relationships depending on whether they recently fought with their partner, or recently had a wonderful weekend together, or are somewhat depressed over having not seen their partner in quite some time. Each of these possibilities has implications for how the results of research are interpreted.

What Do the Research Results Mean?

Perhaps one of the primary concerns with regard to interpretation of findings in research on mate selection is the distinction between actual experience and self-reported preferences. Because virtually all research on the topic is based on self-reports of preferences and retrospective recall of what transpired within respondents' intimate relationships, descriptions of the findings of such research should be couched accordingly. It is more appropriate to conclude that people *reported* certain judgments and opinions to be important in the process of selecting mates, rather than indicating that these are actual values. This may seem like a picky semantic point; however, as has been discussed, peoples' self-reports are vulnerable to various forms of bias and may or may not accurately reflect what occurs in real relationships.

Another potential problem in interpreting research findings has to do with misrepresenting the absolute values of scores or ratings. For example, researchers may conclude that "based on the findings, men are more likely than women to value virginity in a potential mate." Simply reading this conclusion could lead to the assumption that a substantial proportion of men, or even most men, value virginity (and conversely few women do). Of course, one form of potential misrepresentation arises because the statement implies a difference between men and women in general, whereas the finding was based on a particular sample of college students.

Apart from the concern over generalizability of the finding, however, suppose that the conclusion was based on ratings of the characteristic *virgin* as applied to a potential mate and that college student respondents were presented with a seven-point scale for such ratings (where 1 = *Not at All Important* and 7 = *Extremely Important*). The average rating for men might have been 2.43, whereas the mean for women might have been 1.87, and the difference between these means may have been statistically significant. What is missing from the summary statement describing the finding is that the absolute value of both men's and women's ratings indicate that virginity was not particularly important to either sex. It would be more accurate to summarize the finding with the statement that "college students reported that a potential mate's virginity was unimportant, and it was even less so for women respondents than for men respondents." This description is more complicated, but it also helps the reader better understand what the research results actually were. Still, the extent to which such research results help us understand the actual processes of mate selection and sexual decision making is an issue that would require much more extensive investigation.

QUESTIONS FOR DISCUSSION

1. Suppose a friend asked you to describe why you ended up with your current or most recent romantic or sexual partner. That is, what was it about that particular person that led you to have a relationship of this sort with that individual? What would you say? How accurate and complete do you think that answer is when trying to capture the potentially complex process through which the two of you ended up together?
2. Suppose researchers surveyed college students from two settings: sociology classes and bars catering to college students. How might the two samples of college students differ with regard to ratings of how important such characteristics as *religious, fun-loving, wants children,* and *outgoing* are in a potential mate? Would it matter whether the potential mate was to be considered a short-term dating partner or a lifetime partner?
3. Generate some hypotheses, or educated guesses, as to how members within each of the following pairs of samples might differ with regard to what each reports as important in a potential mate: high school students versus college students; individuals who have been married before versus those who have never married; people who have children or want children versus those who do not.

CASE FOR ANALYSIS

Suppose researchers are interested in the mate selection preferences of college students today versus those from previous generations. These researchers locate a published study reporting the results of a survey of college students conducted at a large university in the Midwest during the 1960s. In that study the researchers presented the college students with a list of 10 potential characteristics in a mate and asked students to rank them from most important (1) to least important (10). In the survey conducted in the 1960s, the top-ranked characteristic was "Kind and Understanding." The current researchers decide to administer the same survey (list of 10 characteristics) to students on their campus in Florida. Among these students "Kind and Understanding" ranks third, and "Has Education" ranks first. A reporter from the local newspaper learns of the survey and interviews the researchers. The headline for the resulting newspaper article reads, "College Students Today Value Education More Than in the Past."

PUBLISHED REPORTS FOR FURTHER PRACTICE

Fletcher, G. J. O., Simpson, J. A., Thomas, G., & Giles, L. (1999). Ideals in intimate relationships. *Journal of Personality and Social Psychology, 76*, 72–89.

Herold, E. S., & Milhausen, R. R. (1999). Dating preferences of university women: An analysis of the nice guy stereotype. *Journal of Sex & Marital Therapy, 25*, 333–343.

Lewis, R., Yancey, G., & Bletzer, S. S. (1997). Racial and nonracial factors that influence spouse choice in black/white marriages. *Journal of Black Studies, 28*, 60–78.

McGuirl, K., & Wiederman, M. W. (2000). Characteristics of the ideal sex partner: Gender differences and perceptions of the preferences of the other gender. *Journal of Sex & Marital Therapy, 26*, in press.

Parmer, T. (1998). Characteristics of preferred partners: Variations between African American men and women. *Journal of College Student Development, 39*, 461–471.

Pines, A. M. (1998). A prospective study of personality and gender differences in romantic attraction. *Personality and Individual Differences, 25*, 147–157.

Regan, P. C. (1998). Minimum mate selection standards as a function of perceived mate value, relationship context, and gender. *Journal of Psychology & Human Sexuality, 10*, 53–73.

Regan, P. C., & Berscheid, E. (1997). Gender differences in characteristics desired in a potential sexual and marriage partner. *Journal of Psychology & Human Sexuality, 9*, 25–37.

PROTECTION: HOW FREQUENTLY DO PEOPLE USE CONDOMS?

Given that condoms are an effective method of contraception and for prevention of sexually transmitted diseases (STDs) such as HIV (Reiss & Leik, 1989), knowing the extent to which individuals use condoms is frequently of interest to researchers, educators, and policy makers. The focus of interest may be the prevalence and consistency of condom use within a population in general, or it may be demonstrating that condom use increased after some particular intervention. In either case, the question has to do with prevalence and consistency of a specific behavior—the use of condoms. Such a seemingly simple issue can be challenging to measure accurately.

WAS THE RESEARCH DESIGN ADEQUATE OR APPROPRIATE FOR THE RESEARCH QUESTION?

When the research focus is simply how frequently a behavior is performed, or what percentage of people have performed a particular behavior, the study might be characterized as *descriptive* in nature. The primary purpose of the research is to describe the state of affairs with regard to a certain behavior or experience. In any such study, however, there may be a component that is correlational or experimental, just as a descriptive study may be cross-sectional or longitudinal.

A descriptive study may contain an experimental component in that perhaps the reason for the study is to demonstrate that the rate of a particular behavior, in this case condom use, increases as a result of some intervention (e.g., Guthrie et al., 1996). To demonstrate such an effect, research participants are randomly assigned to an intervention group and a control group, and the rates of condom use in the two groups is compared at some point after completion of the intervention. Researchers could compare rates of condom use in the intervention group at two (or more) points in time without similar comparisons within a control group. However, to do so leaves the researchers questioning whether any observed change might have been due to other factors, such as a pervasive change in the cultural norms or a tendency for people in general to change their condom use behavior over time.

A descriptive study might contain a correlational component such that, in addition to measuring the general rate of condom use, the researchers attempt to determine statistically significant correlates of condom use (e.g., personality characteristics, age, or attitudes). Such studies are typically cross-sectional in that condom use, as well as whatever variables are measured as possible correlates, are assessed at only one point in time (Poppen & Reisen, 1997; Sheeran, Abraham, & Orbell, 1999). Descriptive studies that contain an experimental component are generally longitudinal, as condom use by the same research participants is compared for at least two different points in time. Occasionally researchers measure condom use at different points by drawing a new sample each time from the same population (e.g., Caron, Davis, Wynn, & Roberts, 1992; DeBuono, Zinner, Daamen, & McCormack, 1990). The hope is to assess possible changes over time within that population. However, the cause of any such changes remains unknown, because the samples differ in ways other than just the point in time at which condom use was measured.

WHO WERE THE PARTICIPANTS?

When the primary purpose of research is to reveal the rate of behavior in a particular population, the extent to which the research sample is representative of the population is of utmost importance. Any factor that results in an unrepresentative sample and that may possibly be related to the behavior of interest is a potential problem. For example, researchers interested in the extent of condom use among young adults may sample college students. However, are college students likely to differ from young adults in general in ways that may be related to condom use?

In this case college students could be expected to be better educated and more thoroughly socialized regarding condom use compared to peers who are not college students. Similarly, young adults who are better able to postpone gratification of desires or who are more rational in their decision making may be those young adults most likely to attend college. These characteristics might also be related to an increased likelihood of condom use among college students compared to peers who are not college students. At the same time, college students may have relatively greater access to short-term sexual partners (Maticka-Tyndale & Herold, 1997; Townsend, 1995), or may be more likely to drink alcoholic beverages prior to engaging in sex (Halpern-Felsher, Millstein, & Ellen, 1996), and both factors may lower likelihood of condom use (Lewis, Malow, & Ireland, 1997). Of course, the extent to which these and other factors may affect condom usage among research participants is unknown, but the point is that such factors may have substantial effects when trying to determine how frequently people use condoms.

If the population of focus is gay men, it is important to realize that obtaining a representative sample of gay men is extremely difficult (Blair, 1999). So, any particular research sample is liable to be unique, and the extent to which results generalize to other gay men may be limited. Regardless of sexual orientation, how might rates of condom usage, or the correlates of condom usage, differ among samples recruited from an STD clinic, newspaper advertisements, singles' bars, and church groups? What about high-school students compared to college students compared to older adults? What about respondents from various ethnic groups?

Investigating condom usage among each of these groups may be important in its own right, but it is important to recognize that the results obtained with each may not apply to other types of people. Even within any particular sample, might those who volunteered to participate be more or less likely to use condoms compared to their peers who declined to participate? For example, if researchers sent questionnaires to college students with instructions to return completed questionnaires during the next class meeting, who might be more likely to return the completed questionnaires, those students who use condoms or those who do not? Even if not allowing for embarrassment, perhaps those students who are the most conscientious about returning the questionnaires are the same students who are more conscientious in general, including when it comes to using condoms consistently.

As mentioned earlier, condom usage is often examined within the context of evaluating the effects from participating in some type of intervention (Poppen & Reisen, 1997). Such interventions are typically educational in nature and designed to increase the likelihood or frequency of condom usage among the participants (e.g., National Institute of Mental Health Multisite HIV Prevention Trial Group, 1998). So, participants in some form of educational intervention comprise another type of potential research sample, which entails its own specific concerns regarding generalizability.

Depending on how participants in intervention studies were recruited, they may represent a rather unusual group of highly motivated individuals. For example, if participants were recruited through advertisements describing enrollment in an educational program and no incentive was offered for participation beyond what might be learned in the program, who would be most motivated to enroll? In this case, probably those individuals who already believe that they need to alter their sexual behavior. Because researchers cannot force people to attend, the respondents who actually follow through on their initial interest in the program probably represent the relatively conscientious individuals within the small pool of people initially interested in the program. How might responses regarding condom use differ between those individuals who answer advertisements and actually attend an intervention versus those who were not interested from the start?

Another phenomenon exists among those individuals who do volunteer and actually complete the intervention. Other researchers have shown that when people participate in an intervention, they tend to report that their behavior has been changed in the ways one would expect from such an intervention, even if no change has actually occurred (Dawes, 1988). Participating in an educational program to increase condom usage might result in participants reporting increased usage (perhaps believing that indeed their condom use had increased), even if the program was unsuccessful and had no actual effect on behavior. This may explain why one well-conducted, large-scale intervention resulted in increased reports of condom use, but no change in rate of infection with sexually transmitted disease was documented in the respondents' medical charts (National Institute of Mental Health [NIMH] Multisite HIV Prevention Trial Group, 1998). Of course, this phenomenon is only a concern when the measure of condom use is self-report in nature, which begs the question, "How do researchers typically measure condom use?"

WHAT WERE THE QUESTIONS OR MEASURES USED IN THE RESEARCH?

Condom usage seems straightforward to measure: either condoms are used or they are not used. However, because researchers must rely on self-reports, potential difficulties arise. Unfortunately, researchers have tended to employ just one or two questions to measure condom use, and there has been little consistency across researchers with regard to how condom use has been assessed (Sheeran & Abraham, 1994). One might imagine that individuals who never use condoms or who always use condoms might easily and accurately respond to questions regarding condom usage (Weir, Roddy, Zekeng, Ryan, & Wong, 1998). What about the remaining respondents (perhaps the majority) who occasionally use condoms? How might they recall or estimate condom usage? What factors are likely to influence such recall or estimation?

It is probably the case that individuals have a more difficult time recalling condom usage over long periods of time. So, researchers might have more faith in responses to the question, "Did you use a condom during your most recent experience of vaginal intercourse?" than in responses to the question, "How often did you use condoms during the previous 12 months?" In responding to this latter question, an individual who recently has been using condoms consistently might tend to overestimate condom usage for the past year compared to someone who had used them quite regularly but who has been lax over the past few months. In actuality both individuals might have had the same condom usage rates over the past year, but their more recent experience biases their estimates of behavior over the long span of time.

Even the response choices respondents are given can influence the data research participants provide. Researchers typically provide respondents with a response scale anchored from "never" to "always" with regard to condom use (Sheeran & Abraham, 1994). It is easy to imagine that there is variation across respondents in how each interprets intermediate points on the scale, such as those that might be labeled "rarely," "occasionally," "sometimes," or "frequently." However, even with regard to the more definite terms "always" and "never" there is apparently individual variation in how these terms are applied to condom use. Cecil and Zimet (1998) found that a substantial proportion (more than 50%) of college student respondents interpreted using condoms 18 or 19 times out of 20 as "always" and using condoms once or twice out 20 times as "never."

Since public recognition of HIV, numerous media campaigns have been implemented to promote condom use as the responsible choice when engaging in sexual intercourse, so using condoms is a socially desirable behavior in contemporary Western culture (Agnew & Loving, 1998). As a result, when researchers ask respondents about condom use, one concern is that respondents will tend to overestimate or overreport such behavior (Jeannin et al., 1998). To underreport or to admit to not using condoms might imply that the respondent is irresponsible or reckless with regard to his or her own health as well as that of his or her sexual partners.

The more socially desirable a particular behavior, the more likely respondents may be to overreport the behavior when asked under conditions when not having done so would be embarrassing. Because condom use is socially approved, and admitting that one does not use condoms could be difficult because of what it might imply, it might be easiest to admit not using condoms when the question is posed under anonymous conditions. Conversely, if respondents are being personally interviewed or believe that their responses are not anonymous, researchers might expect the greatest tendency to overestimate or overreport condom use.

Providing socially desirable answers might be of greatest concern when researchers ask respondents to provide an indication of past behavioral change or future intentions to use condoms. Several research projects have been based on such estimates of past behavior change (e.g., Ishii-Kuntz, Whitbeck, & Simons, 1990; Jurich, Adams, & Schulenberg, 1992; Melnick et al., 1993) or future condom use (e.g., Agnew & Loving, 1998; Agocha & Cooper, 1999; Rosenthal, Fernbach, & Moore, 1997). One should be skeptical of peoples' reports regarding how they have changed or how they intend to change, both of which are easy to claim (remember those New Year's resolutions?). In fact, what would it imply about the respondent if he or she claimed *not* to have changed sexual behavior to reduce risk or that he or she does *not* intend to use condoms with new partners? If there is little faith in the primary measure of condom use a particular group of researchers use, the question of what the research results mean is of great importance.

WHAT DO THE RESEARCH RESULTS MEAN?

If researchers conclude that "only 25% of individuals use condoms consistently," several questions remain. Who were the respondents, and are the results with this group of individuals likely to generalize to the larger population from which respondents were drawn? When researchers say "use condoms," how was such behavior measured? Most likely the answer includes self-reports. So, to what extent might the proportion of respondents who reported condom use be an overestimate or underestimate of the proportion who actually do use condoms? What do the researchers mean by the term *consistently*? Was this term included in the questions respondents answered regarding their own condom use? If so, might various respondents have interpreted the term differently? If the term was not included in questions posed to respondents, how did the researchers define *consistently* compared to the questions actually presented? What responses by research participants do the researchers consider to indicate "consistent" condom use?

One might be especially concerned of results based on self-reports from individuals who underwent some type of intervention, or who provided responses under conditions other than total anonymity. In both cases, reported condom use (or degree of past behavioral change or future intentions to use condoms) is liable to be overreported, because respondents are likely to believe that their condom use should have increased (or will increase) or that it would be embarrassing to admit not having changed their behavior.

Of course, no single research study is perfect, especially when researchers must rely on self-reports of sensitive behavior such as condom use. Still, thinking critically about research means recognizing the limitations of each study and interpreting the results in light of such limitations.

QUESTIONS FOR DISCUSSION

1. If research participants are asked whether they "use condoms consistently," what are the various ways respondents might interpret this phrase? How might the various interpretations influence the answers respondents provide?
2. If you were interested in measuring the frequency or consistency with which people use condoms, how might you best word your question(s) to

elicit the most meaningful response? Can you think of a way to measure condom use without relying on self-report? What would be the advantages and disadvantages of this alternative?

3. Suppose your goal was to demonstrate rather high rates of condom use among college students. How might you sample students or recruit research participants to help ensure that your results were consistent with your goal? What about if your goal was to illustrate a high degree of sexual irresponsibility (low condom use) among college students?

CASE FOR ANALYSIS

Suppose researchers hypothesize that presenting condom use in a positive light would be an effective strategy for increasing condom use among young adults. These researchers noticed how educational films on condom use often take a scare tactic approach by emphasizing all of the negative things that may result from not using condoms. The researchers obtain one such film intended for college student audiences and also produce their own film in which the benefits of using condoms are clearly the focus.

To examine the effects of their new video, the researchers elicit the help of several colleagues who teach a variety of courses on campus. These instructors pass out an anonymous questionnaire containing the question, "In what proportion of future sexual encounters do you intend to use a condom?" (0–100%). The courses these instructors teach are then randomly assigned to one of three conditions: 1) viewing the negative condom film, 2) viewing the positive condom film, or 3) viewing a film on gender roles in Western culture (control condition). After each film the students are asked to again complete the anonymous questionnaire. The researchers find that the proportion of sexual encounters in which condom use was intended increased in both condom film conditions but not the control condition, and the greatest increase was found in the positive condom film condition. After a reporter for the campus newspaper interviews one of the researchers, a headline reads, "Power of the Positive Spin: Positive Message Increases Condom Use." The article goes on to explain that the results of the research reveal that both negative and positive condom films are effective, but positive films result in the greatest increase in condom use.

PUBLISHED REPORTS FOR FURTHER PRACTICE

Civic, D., (2000). College students' reasons for nonuse of condoms within dating relationships. *Journal of Sex & Marital Therapy, 26,* 95–105.

Kusseling, F. S., Shapiro, M. F., Greenberg, J. M., & Wenger, N. S. (1996). Understanding why heterosexual adults do not practice safer sex: A comparison of two samples. *AIDS Education and Prevention, 8*, 247–257.

McNair, L. D., Carter, J. A., & Williams, M. K. (1998). Self-esteem, gender, and alcohol use: Relationships with HIV risk perception and behaviors in college students. *Journal of Sex & Marital Therapy, 24*, 29–36.

Polacsek, M., Celentano, D. D., O'Campo, P., & Santelli, J. (1999). Correlates of condom use stage of change: Implications for intervention. *AIDS Education and Prevention, 11*, 38–52.

Rosenthal, D., Fernbach, M., & Moore, S. (1997). The singles scene: Safe sex practices and attitudes among at-risk heterosexual adults. *Psychology and Health, 12*, 171–182.

Schuster, C. (1997). Condom use behavior: An assessment of United States college students' health education needs. *International Quarterly of Community Health Education, 17*, 237–254.

Tigges, B. B., Wills, T. A., & Link, B. G. (1998). Social comparison, the threat of AIDS, and adolescent condom use. *Journal of Applied Social Psychology, 28*, 861–887.

Weinberg, M. S., Lottes, I. L., & Aveline, D. (1998). AIDS risk-reduction strategies among United States and Swedish heterosexual university students. *Archives of Sexual Behavior, 27*, 385–401.

INFIDELITY: WHAT PROPORTION OF PEOPLE HAVE HAD EXTRADYADIC SEX?

In contemporary Western culture there are strong norms regarding monogamy and sexual exclusivity. Americans typically report the belief that it is only acceptable to be involved in one sexual relationship at a time and that sexual contact with someone outside of the primary dyad (couple) is wrong (Laumann et al., 1994; Wiederman, 1997a). One might refer to such sexual involvement as *extramarital* if the primary partners are married to one another, or use the more generic term *extradyadic sex* to refer to sexual activity with someone other than one's primary romantic partner (who may be a spouse or dating partner).

Discovery that one relationship partner has engaged in extradyadic sex while involved in a presumably exclusive relationship can lead to jealousy and emotional upset (Wiederman & Allgeier, 1993; Wright, 1999), as well as harm and a possible end to the primary relationship (Charny & Parnass, 1995; Shackelford, 1998; Wiederman & Allgeier, 1996). Given the social prohibitions and the possible harm extradyadic sex can cause one's primary relationship, one might assume that extradyadic sex is rare. However, occasionally statistics are offered from the various media claiming that "half of married people have extramarital sex," or some similar "fact." How much credibility should be given such claims, even when they are attributed to empirical research?

WAS THE RESEARCH DESIGN ADEQUATE OR APPROPRIATE FOR THE RESEARCH QUESTION?

When the research focus is simply what percentage of people have performed a particular behavior, the study might be said to be *descriptive* in nature. That is, the primary purpose of the research is to describe the state of affairs with regard to a certain behavior or experience; in this case, extradyadic sex. There may be a correlational aspect to the research, as the investigators attempt to discover what characteristics of individuals or relationships are related to increased likelihood of extradyadic sex (e.g., Glass & Wright, 1992; Wiederman & Allgeier, 1996). Such studies, however, are typically cross-sectional, and their primary focus is on determining the proportion of respondents who have had extradyadic sexual experience (e.g., Wiederman, 1997a; Wiederman & Hurd, 1999; Yarab, Sensibaugh, & Allgeier, 1998). Accordingly, the primary concerns in these types of studies are the representativeness of the sample (or the generalizability of the results) as well as how the construct (extradyadic sex) is measured.

WHO WERE THE PARTICIPANTS?

Imagine an extreme example in which researchers interested in examining the prevalence of extramarital sex place advertisements in newspapers recruiting individuals who have had such experience. This method of participant recruitment would be useless for determining the prevalence of extramarital sex because only those individuals with such experience would be likely to contact the researchers. Of course, trained researchers would not fall prey to such an obvious methodological problem. However, similar self-selection factors may occur in other forms of participant recruitment, and these factors may result in a distorted perspective on the prevalence of extradyadic sex.

In the 1970s several researchers conducted large-scale surveys examining the prevalence of extramarital sex (Hite, 1976, 1983; Hunt, 1974; Tavris & Sadd, 1975). The results of these surveys led some writers to conclude that at least half of married men, and nearly as many married women, engaged in extramarital sex (e.g., see Thompson, 1983). In contrast, data collected in the early 1990s revealed that, among those who had ever been married, approximately 11–15% of women and 19–25% of men in the United States reported having had extramarital sex (Clements, 1994; Laumann et al., 1994; Wiederman, 1997a). Why the discrepancy? If all one knew were the results mentioned here, it might be tempting to conclude that Americans became less likely to engage in extramarital sex from the 1970s to the 1990s. However, understanding these findings rests on examining the methods of sampling the researchers used.

The earlier surveys that resulted in relatively high rates of extramarital sex were conducted with convenience samples. That is, no attempt was made to select a nationally representative sample; rather, potential respondents were recruited through whatever means were convenient. Accordingly, questionnaires were published in men's magazines, such as *Playboy* and *Penthouse*, or women's magazines, such as *Redbook*, sent to respondents who requested them after reading about previous research results published by the researchers or after encountering the researchers discussing earlier results on television, and so forth. The resulting rates of extramarital sex were generally quite high, and in some cases the majority of respondents reported having had extramarital sex.

The more recent large-scale surveys were each based on nationally representative samples in which great care was taken to assure that the respondents in the final sample mirrored the larger United States population with regard to such basic demographic variables as age, ethnicity, and size of resident city (Clements, 1994; Laumann et al., 1994; Wiederman, 1997a). To obtain such samples, investigators could not rely on potential respondents to contact the researchers but rather had to systematically select potential respondents and then attempt to persuade them to participate in the survey. Why might rates of extramarital sex differ widely between surveys based on convenience samples and those based on nationally representative samples?

The answer might be found by first asking what types of individuals would be most likely to encounter, and then respond to, recruitment attempts in the research projects described from the 1970s. Because a primary method of data collection in those surveys involved publishing the questionnaires in magazines, individuals who were not readers of those particular magazines would not encounter the questionnaires and would be unable to participate. Might readers of *Playboy*, *Penthouse*, and *Redbook* be expected to differ in their sexual attitudes and experiences compared to Americans in general? Might they differ from the larger population even with regard to such basic demographic variables as age? If so, how might the results from these individuals provide a distorted view of what people in general experience sexually?

The respondents to these early surveys were not even representative of the readers of the magazines in which the surveys were published. Importantly, only a small fraction of the questionnaires distributed in those magazines were actually returned to the researchers. Might those readers who took the time to complete the survey and return it differ in significant ways from those readers who did not? One might imagine, for example, that those respondents who had more sexual experiences, and perhaps more varied and unusual experiences, may have been most likely to respond. These individuals not only may have been most comfortable with sexual issues, but they also may have been most likely to believe they had something worthwhile or interesting to report. In the end, one may assume that survey results based on such convenience methods will tend to be distorted toward those who have relatively greater sexual experience (in this case extramarital experience) and relatively more liberal sexual attitudes.

What about college student samples? Several investigators have examined the prevalence of extradyadic sex during dating, each employing college student samples (Hansen, 1987; Roscoe, Cavanaugh, & Kennedy, 1988; Sheppard, Nelson, & Andreoli-Mathie, 1995; Wiederman & Hurd, 1999; Yarab et al., 1998). One might imagine how college students might differ from noncollege students of the same age with regard to extradyadic sex. For example, college provides a ready-made social environment of like-minded peers, complete with parties, bars, and social organizations and clubs. Also, college students typically are not living with their parents and are often not even living in their hometown, yet frequently have a primary relationship partner who lives in their hometown or who attends college elsewhere. Accordingly, college students may experience greater freedom and opportunity to experiment sexually relative to their peers who did not go to college. These and other factors might result in a greater proportion of college students engaging in extradyadic sex compared to peers who are not college students. Even among studies based on college student respondents, however, might results vary across similar samples?

Hansen (1987) surveyed students enrolled in sociology classes, whereas Wiederman and Hurd (1999), Yarab et al. (1998), and Sheppard et al. (1995) each surveyed students enrolled in psychology courses (Roscoe et al. [1988] did not report such information). Even though all of these researchers administered anonymous questionnaires to seemingly similar college student samples, the methods of recruitment, incentives for participation, and the conditions under which respondents completed the measures varied.

Respondents in Hansen's and Sheppard et al.'s study completed the questionnaires in class, respondents in Yarab et al.'s study took questionnaires home to complete and return to the instructor during the next class meeting, and participants in Wiederman and Hurd's study were recruited through an introductory psychology research participant pool in which respondents did not know the nature of the research until arriving at a designated testing site. The research participants in Yarab et al.'s study and Wiederman and Hurd's study received credit toward their psychology course, whereas the students in Hansen's and Sheppard et al.'s study apparently were not compensated or given any incentive for participation.

How might these methodological variations have affected the representativeness of the sample obtained or the responses research participants gave? Consider, for example, that in Yarab et al.'s study, 8% of the students returned the questionnaire blank and another 6% were not included in the final sample because of missing data or failure to follow instructions in completing the questionnaire. Might these 14% of potential respondents have differed in their experiences with extradyadic sex compared to the majority who completed the measures and were included in the sample? If the answer to that question could be "yes," might they have been more or less likely than the remaining students to have had extradyadic sexual experience?

In addition to variation in the methods of recruitment and the conditions under which respondents participate in the research, studies of extradyadic sex have also varied with regard to measurement of extradyadic sexual experience. Just as variation in participant recruitment can affect results, so too can the way questions are asked or response choices provided.

WHAT WERE THE QUESTIONS OR MEASURES USED IN THE RESEARCH?

What constitutes extradyadic or extramarital sex? The answer may seem straightforward because it is likely that you have a notion for what behaviors and contexts would be inappropriate to you. The difficulty lies in the fact that people vary in their definitions of terms and what exactly qualifies as extradyadic sex. At the start of this chapter I implied that sexual activity with someone other than the primary partner while sexually or romantically involved with that primary partner might constitute extradyadic sex. However, how are *sexual activity* and *primary partner* to be defined? Does kissing someone other than your primary partner constitute extradyadic sex, or do genitals have to be involved? What about only engaging in oral sex? What about oral sex given but not received, or received but not given?

In this definition of extradyadic sex, does *primary partner* include someone whom you have been dating but with whom you have not discussed the issue of dating others? Does *primary partner* include a spouse from whom you are separated and planning to divorce? Does it matter whether your primary partner engaged in extradyadic sex first, and you engaged in extradyadic sex during the period when you were fighting with your primary partner? With regard to labeling your behavior as extradyadic sex, does it matter whether your extradyadic partner is a stranger, a prostitute, or a former lover, or whether there was any emotional involvement at all? Across individuals there is likely to be at least some variation in the answers to these and other, similar questions.

So, if respondents are asked whether each has engaged in extradyadic sex, or worse still, whether each has been "unfaithful" (see Roscoe et al., 1988; Sheppard et al., 1995), the responses will necessarily vary depending on each respondent's definition of the terms. For example, when previous researchers asked college students what constitutes being unfaithful to a dating partner, a wide range of behaviors were reported, including sexual contact with an extradyadic partner, simply spending time with someone other than one's primary partner, becoming emotionally close to someone else, keeping secrets from one's partner, having fantasies about someone else, and flirting, studying, or dancing with someone other than the primary partner (Roscoe et al., 1988; Sheppard et al., 1995; Yarab et al., 1998).

Beyond potential problems with definition of terms, the wording of questions can affect whether respondents are willing to admit to particular experiences or even to see themselves as a particular type of person. Imagine how responses might differ to the following two questions, each of which may have been designed to measure the same thing:

1. *Have you ever been sexually unfaithful or engaged in infidelity within a dating relationship?*

2. *Many times people are involved in a romantic relationship with one person but still experience attraction to others. Situations may arise in which such feelings are acted upon. Have you ever been involved in an ongoing, serious relationship with one person, yet had some form of sexual contact with someone other than your primary partner?*

Both of these questions contain ambiguities with regard to terms and possible definitions. However, the first question may be more open to interpretation, and it certainly implies that the behavior being asked about is less common and inappropriate. Because the first question asks about infidelity without necessarily specifying that it has to include extradyadic sexual activity, some people might answer "no" to the second question but "yes" to the first question (e.g., perhaps they had sexual fantasies about someone other than their primary partner). Similarly, some respondents may have had an experience that fits with the behavior being asked about in the second question, but because of the circumstances under which the behavior occurred, the respondent does not consider it to have been an act of infidelity or a case of being unfaithful (e.g., Jenks, 1998; Wheeler & Kilmann, 1983). These respondents might answer "no" to the first question but "yes" to the second.

I noted that extradyadic sex is a socially undesirable behavior in contemporary Western culture because it violates the exclusivity norms that people report believing in (Wiederman, 1997a). To admit having engaged in extradyadic sex implies that one was unfaithful, selfish, and cannot be trusted. So, another important question to raise in evaluating research on the topic is, What incentive did respondents have to be accurate and truthful? Did they respond under conditions that might compromise their honesty? Certainly if respondents were asked whether each had engaged in extradyadic sex, and the spouse or primary partner was present to hear or see the answer, it would be doubtful that the resulting proportion of people who admit to having had extradyadic sex is even close to the proportion who actually have. Even in an anonymous telephone interview, the respondent may have little incentive for admitting to extradyadic sex, because they may have lingering doubts as to whether the survey is legitimate and whether the interview is truly anonymous.

Despite limitations in any particular research project, researchers will end up with a prevalence rate for extradyadic sex. Just what that particular rate means with regard to peoples' actual experience is worth considering in its own right.

WHAT DO THE RESEARCH RESULTS MEAN?

"The majority of Americans will experience extramarital sex." You may encounter a similar conclusion presented in the media at some point, if you have not already. After having considered some of the relevant issues when conducting research on people's experience of extradyadic sex, such a conclusion should raise several questions.

The prevalence rate given by any particular set of researchers is liable to be higher or lower than the actual rate in the population, depending on how respondents were sampled, the way questions were asked, and the conditions under which individuals were asked to respond. These issues are important to consider not only when evaluating the results of a new study but also when attempting to determine whether behavior within a culture has changed over time. If researchers conclude that extradyadic sexual activity has increased or decreased, it is important to consider the multiple ways in which the studies being compared may have differed that would account for corresponding differences in results.

What's more, prevalence rates do not tell us anything about the meanings people attach to extradyadic sex and the various behaviors that might be included (Atwood & Seifer, 1997; Levine, 1998; Wiederman & Allgeier, 1996), nor about the possible variations across ethnic groups (Penn, Hernandez, & Bermudez, 1997). To examine these and other issues, researchers and those who evaluate their conclusions need to be sensitive to issues of sampling, terminology and question wording, and interpretation of results.

QUESTIONS FOR DISCUSSION

1. There are probably some people who have engaged in extradyadic sexual activity that most people would consider to have been an act of infidelity, yet they themselves do not consider it so. Why might these individuals disagree with the majority? How might they go about convincing themselves or others that their action was not infidelity?

2. What methods of sampling or recruiting research participants would likely result in a relatively high proportion of individuals indicating extradyadic sexual activity? What about a relatively low incidence?

3. Past research has demonstrated that men are more likely than women to indicate having engaged in some form of extradyadic sexual activity both before marriage (Wiederman & Hurd, 1999) and after marriage (Wiederman, 1997a). Generate as many reasons as you can why this might be the case. How many of your reasons have to do with actual male-female

differences in the incidence of extradyadic sexual activity, versus male-female differences in the likelihood of recalling, labeling, and reporting certain experiences?

CASE FOR ANALYSIS

Suppose researchers are interested in the incidence of extramarital sex as a function of age. These researchers employ a nationally representative sample of adults, ages 18 years and older and ask each one whether he or she "has ever experienced extramarital sex." Because extramarital sex can occur only among those who are married, people who are selected for inclusion in the sample but who are not currently married are not asked the question. The researchers find that, among the men, the older respondents in the sample are *most* likely to report having engaged in extramarital sex, whereas among women, the oldest respondents are *least* likely to report extramarital sex. After publication of the findings in a peer-reviewed journal, a magazine reporter writes a brief article about the findings. In the article the reporter writes, "The findings of this latest study indicate that young women today are more likely to have extramarital sex than they were in the past, and the opposite pattern was found for men."

PUBLISHED REPORTS FOR FURTHER PRACTICE

Buss, D. M., & Shackelford, T. K. (1997). Susceptibility to infidelity in the first year of marriage. *Journal of Research in Personality, 31*, 193–221.

Buunk, B. P., & Bakker, A. B. (1995). Extradyadic sex: The role of descriptive and injunctive norms. *The Journal of Sex Research, 32*, 313–318.

Choi, K., Catania, J. A., & Dolcini, M. M. (1994). Extramarital sex and HIV risk behavior among US adults: Results from the National AIDS Behavioral Survey. *American Journal of Public Health, 84*, 2003–2007.

Forste, R., & Tanfer, K. (1996). Sexual exclusivity among dating, cohabiting, and married women. *Journal of Marriage and the Family, 58*, 33–47.

Sheppard, V. J., Nelson, E. S., & Andreoli-Mathie, V. (1995). Dating relationships and infidelity: Attitudes and behavior. *Journal of Sex & Marital Therapy, 21*, 202–212.

Wiederman, M. W. (1997). Extramarital sex: Prevalence and correlates in a national survey. *The Journal of Sex Research, 34*, 167–174.

Wiederman, M. W., & Hurd, C. (1999). Extradyadic involvement during dating. *Journal of Social and Personal Relationships, 16*, 265–274.

Yarab, P. E., Sensibaugh, C. C., & Allgeier, E. R. (1998). More than just sex: Gender differences in the incidence of self-defined unfaithful behavior in heterosexual dating relationships. *Journal of Psychology & Human Sexuality, 10*, 45–57.

ORIENTATION: WHAT DETERMINES SEXUAL ATTRACTION TO MEN OR WOMEN?

Virtually everyone will experience sexual attraction toward others, at least at some point in life (McClintock & Herdt, 1996). Many people experience such attraction several times each day (Jones & Barlow, 1990). What determines whether we are attracted sexually to men, to women, or to both men and women? People often refer to the answer to this question as one's *sexual orientation* (Sell, 1997). Despite being something that is central to peoples' experience, we know relatively little regarding the determinants of individuals' sexual orientation. As this chapter will reveal, the concept of sexual orientation is a slippery one, and conducting research on sexual orientation is difficult.

WAS THE RESEARCH DESIGN ADEQUATE OR APPROPRIATE FOR THE RESEARCH QUESTION?

Because the research question has to do with what determines people's sexual orientation, in principle only experimental research can address the issue. The primary causes of sexual orientation that have been proposed generally fall into one of two broad categories: genetic, or biological, causes (e.g., Diamond, 1993, 1998) versus social, or learned, causes (e.g., Rosenbluth, 1997). Unfortunately, to perform an experiment by systematically manipulating the relevant factors in either of these areas would be unethical and probably impossible. Experimental tests of biological explanations would involve prenatal alteration of genetic material or prenatal exposure to hormones. Experimental tests of learning explanations would involve systematically exposing children to certain stimuli and experiences to determine later whether their adult sexual orientation is affected. Because such experiments cannot be conducted, research into the determinants of sexual orientation is correlational in nature. Ultimately, then, issues of causality are difficult to establish.

74

To consider possible biological, or genetic, causes first, there has been a good deal of emphasis on these theories in an attempt to explain sexual orientation (Bailey & Pillard, 1995; Ellis & Ebertz, 1997; Gladue, 1994; Hamer & Copeland, 1994). Much of the research in this area has focused on either differences in hormonal levels or on structural differences in brains among people of varying sexual orientations (Byne & Parsons, 1993; Ellis & Ames, 1987; Schklenk & Ristow, 1996). If researchers find such differences, they often hypothesize that these are the causes of orientation, or at least are signs of the underlying biological causes of orientation (Hamer & Copeland, 1994; LeVay, 1996). This line of reasoning rests on the assumption that anatomical structures and hormonal levels precede sexual feelings and behaviors. However, other research illustrates how behavior and experience can also influence neurochemistry and the development of neuroanatomical structures (Goleman, 1995; Grober, 1998). So, it is unclear whether any anatomical and neurochemical factors associated with sexual orientation are a cause or an effect of sexual orientation, or perhaps simply a correlate of sexual orientation (the biological factors and sexual orientation may be both caused by some third variable).

Another strategy for examining the possible genetic underpinnings of sexual orientation involves studying identical twins. Since they share all of their genes, whereas typical siblings do not, if sexual orientation has a genetic component, then the sexual orientation of identical twins should be the same with greater frequency than among typical siblings. Genetic theories of sexual orientation predict that if a member of an identical twin pair is gay or lesbian, that person's twin should be much more likely to be gay or lesbian compared to the non-twin sibling of that individual or the non-twin siblings of other gay or lesbian individuals. So, some researchers perform "twin studies" and examine the correspondence of sexual orientation within sibling pairs, comparing those pairs that are identical twins to other sibling pairs (Bailey, Dunn, & Martin, 2000).

With regard to social, or learning, factors that have been proposed as determinants of sexual orientation, researchers typically look for experiences that distinguish respondents of various sexual orientations. These experiences are often believed to have occurred during childhood or adolescence (e.g., Bailey & Zucker, 1995; Rottnek, 1999). The underlying assumption is that, because expression of sexual orientation typically does not emerge until adolescence or young adulthood, experiences during childhood that differ for individuals of one sexual orientation compared to others might be a cause of the subsequent sexual feelings and attractions. However, even if particular childhood experiences or characteristics do occur more frequently among people with one type of sexual orientation compared to people with another type, the direction of causality is unknown. Also, there is always the possibility that sexual orientation and the childhood characteristics are correlated because both are caused by the same other variable (e.g., perhaps some biological difference; Berenbaum & Snyder, 1995). Research on sexual orientation is further complicated by the issue of securing adequate samples of participants.

WHO WERE THE PARTICIPANTS?

Examining determinants of sexual orientation requires comparing people with different orientations (e.g., straight versus bisexual versus gay or lesbian individuals). Although a layperson may typically conceive of individuals as forming clearly defined groups based on sexual orientation, actually categorizing people for research purposes is a controversial task (Sell, 1997; Hewitt, 1998). First, researchers need to decide how they are going to define sexual orientation. For example, will it be based on the sex of the individuals with whom each research participant has shared sexual activity? Will it be based on the sex of the individuals each research participant feels sexual attraction toward, regardless of whether he or she has acted on such feelings? In either case, do researchers determine the participants' sexual orientation based on questions as to sexual feelings and experiences, or do researchers ask respondents to label their own sexual orientation? As it will become clear, each choice has both advantages and limitations, and none of them stand out as the clear winner.

Even during the relatively short era from when sexual orientation was first studied until the present, ways of defining or measuring sexual orientation have varied widely (Sell, 1997). For example, Kinsey and his colleagues (1948, 1953) recognized that people do not always fit neatly into discrete categories, such as heterosexual, bisexual, and homosexual. Accordingly, they developed a seven-point continuum along which each respondent was considered to fall. One end of the continuum was anchored with 0 and was meant to represent people who had no same-gender physical contacts that resulted in erotic arousal or orgasm, and who also had no erotic emotional responses to members of the same gender. The other end of the continuum was labeled with a 6 and was meant to represent those individuals who had only sexual activity and feelings involving members of the same gender. In between these extremes were five points representing mixtures of heterosexual and homosexual experience and emotional responses (see Sell, 1997, Figure 2 for the scale). Some subsequent researchers continued to use Kinsey's scale, whereas others have defined sexual orientation differently. How researchers conceptualize sexual orientation will determine who ends up being the focus of study.

Suppose that researchers base notions of sexual orientation on sexual experience: those who have had sexual experience only with members of the other gender are categorized as heterosexual, those who have had sexual contact with members of both genders are categorized as bisexual, and those who have had sexual contact only with members of the same gender are categorized as homosexual. Once *sexual contact* is defined, such a system seems quite clear. However, in practice the users of such a system encounter problems. For example, having some form of sexual contact with members of the same gender may be a common aspect of childhood or adolescent development in contemporary Western culture, even though most such individuals grow up to behave and label themselves heterosexual (Lamb & Coakley, 1993; Okami, Olmstead, & Abramson, 1997). Also, what about differences between people who have same-gender sexual contact because that is what they prefer versus those who do so out of curiosity or because they have limited access to partners (Hewitt, 1998)?

Because of the many possibilities that exist, some adults who have sexual contact with members of their own gender may maintain that they are heterosexual (Hencken, 1984; Kitzinger & Wilkinson, 1995). Conversely, many (if not most) women who currently consider themselves lesbian report having had sexual relationships with men, and some will apparently do so in their future (Kitzinger & Wilkinson, 1995; Rothblum, 1994). What about men and women who consider themselves gay, lesbian, or bisexual (perhaps based on feelings and fantasies) but who have not had sexual contact with a person of the same gender?

The previous paragraphs presented the difficulties inherent in defining sexual orientation according to behavior, as the behavior may not coincide with self-identity (Hewitt, 1998). However, there are similar problems with defining sexual orientation according to self-labeling. Perhaps because of societal stigma associated with the label "homosexual," some individuals who fit a behavioral definition of gay or lesbian do not identify themselves as such (Kitzinger & Wilkinson, 1995; Hencken, 1984). Also, some individuals who have had sexual relationships with both men and women may label themselves "bisexual," whereas others with similar experiences may label themselves heterosexual or homosexual, perhaps dismissing those experiences as "just going through a phase."

The issue of determining sexual orientation is even more cloudy when researchers must rely on reports from family members regarding the sexual orientation of their relatives. In some studies of sexual orientation, respondents are asked to report on the sexual orientation of other family members (siblings, cousins) so that the researchers can construct a family tree based on sexual orientation (Kirk, Bailey, & Martin, 1999). Of course these reports may be less than accurate, since the respondent is asked to make judgments about the sexual orientation of others. Indeed, Kirk et al. (1999) compared the judgments of respondents regarding their siblings' sexual orientation to the self-reports of those siblings and found some disagreement.

What are the sampling implications of a researcher's choice of definitions for sexual orientation? Given the social stigma associated with the label "homosexual," as well as the low incidence of gay and lesbian individuals in the population, trying to obtain a fairly large, representative sample of gay or lesbian individuals is extremely difficult (Blair, 1999). As a result, researchers often rely on convenience samples and try to recruit research participants through channels that are likely to target nonheterosexual individuals. For example, researchers may attempt to locate such individuals by surveying members of gay and lesbian rights groups or social groups organized by gay, lesbian, or bisexual members (Sandfort, 1997). Might these individuals differ in important ways from others who would self-identify as gay, lesbian, or bisexual but who do not belong to such organizations? Those who openly belong to gay- or lesbian-identified groups are probably the most comfortable with labeling themselves as gay or lesbian and confronting cultural stigma and discrimination (Rothblum, 1994; Sandfort, 1997).

The forms of selection bias discussed so far also have important implications for twin studies examining the genetic contribution to sexual orientation. Until recently, all such twin studies relied on samples recruited through social networks of nonheterosexual individuals, publications targeted to gay, lesbian, and bisexual readers, and word of mouth (Bailey et al., 2000). It is likely that samples of twins recruited in this manner result in overestimates of the genetic contribution to sexual orientation, because twin pairs who share a non-heterosexual orientation are probably more likely to volunteer to participate than are twins who do not correspond with regard to sexual orientation. Bailey et al. (2000) examined the rate of correspondence for sexual orientation among a national sample of nearly 5,000 twins. They found a much lower rate of similarity of sexual orientation among the identical twins in their sample than previous researchers had found in convenience samples.

WHAT WERE THE QUESTIONS OR MEASURES USED IN THE RESEARCH?

As discussed above, in attempting to measure respondents' sexual orientation, researchers may focus on previous sexual experiences. However, doing so raises the question of whether sexual activity, particularly when asked about in questionnaires, is comparable across the various possible pairings of male and female participants. For example, what is lesbian sexual activity (Rothblum, 1994)? If researchers asked female respondents whether each had ever experienced sexual contact with another female, how might the various respondents interpret the term *sexual contact*? Suppose that the researchers were more careful to define sexual contact as somehow involving the genitals. One potential problem is that many lesbian relationships may involve affection and sexual expression with little, if any, focus on the genitals (Kitzinger & Wilkinson, 1995; Rothblum, 1994).

Researchers may attempt to compare the developmental experiences of people classified as homosexual, bisexual, and heterosexual in hopes of establishing differences that may indicate possible causes of sexual orientation. Ideally, researchers would measure the variables of interest during childhood and then follow research participants over time to learn what sexual orientations emerge across participants. Such longitudinal research is costly, however, and when a small proportion of individuals in a population develop a nonheterosexual orientation, large numbers of respondents are needed to create comparison groups of appropriate size.

Instead of performing longitudinal research, investigators often simply ask respondents to recall and report childhood and adolescent experiences (Bailey, Nothnagel, & Wolfe, 1995; Bailey & Zucker, 1995; McClintock & Herdt, 1996). Chapter 4 outlined the potential problems with such retrospective reports, including the inaccuracies that are often inherent. In the context of studying sexual orientation, who might be most likely to selectively remember or distort early experiences that seem to coincide with developing a nonheterosexual orientation? It may be that those research participants who are most comfortable with self-identifying as gay or lesbian or bisexual are also the ones most likely to remember and report particular developmental experiences. Other research participants may have had similar experiences, yet because they self-identify as heterosexual, they either do not recall or do not report having had such experiences. Of course, any time research results are based on retrospective self-reports researchers should be cautious as to the interpretation of those results.

WHAT DO THE RESEARCH RESULTS MEAN?

It is likely that the development of sexual orientation is a complex process involving both biological and social factors (e.g., Bem, 1996; Byne & Parsons, 1993; McClintock & Herdt, 1996). No one factor, gene, or experience can be counted on to accurately predict people's sexual orientation. At the same time, there is the possibility that different individuals arrive at a particular sexual orientation through different pathways (Byne & Parsons, 1993). If this is the case, then perhaps just about any plausible explanation for the development of sexual orientation will accurately describe at least some individuals.

Researchers examining a single factor or a small set of factors may find some support for their hypotheses, yet that does not mean that they have explained the development of sexual orientation for everyone (or even for most people). So, the first question when interpreting findings has to do with their practical significance. If the variables the researchers examined determine sexual orientation for at least some people, what proportion of individuals might be accurately described according to these variables? Note in this context that simply finding that two groups (e.g., heterosexuals and homosexuals) exhibit a statistically significant difference with regard to some variables does not mean that the groups are entirely distinct with regard to those variables. It is likely that the distribution of the variables overlaps between the two groups. So, how do the researchers explain those heterosexual individuals who score similarly to members of the homosexual group, and vice versa (Byne & Parsons, 1993)? Are these instances or possibilities glossed over or ignored?

Ultimately, because much of the research on sexual orientation contains at least some aspect that is based on self-report, and because all such research is correlational in nature, care should be taken when drawing a conclusion about causality. Perhaps in no other area of sexuality research is there greater potential for correlations between two variables to be explained by their being caused by a third variable or set of variables. For example, adults of different sexual orientations may indeed differ reliably with regard to particular childhood experiences, but it is still not known whether those experiences played a causal role in the development of sexual orientation or whether both the childhood experiences and the adult sexual orientation were caused by some underlying variable (e.g., prenatal influences on the structure or organization of the brain).

QUESTIONS FOR DISCUSSION

1. Other than those discussed in the chapter, can you think of a way researchers could go about efficiently recruiting a fairly sizable sample of individuals who identify as gay, lesbian, or bisexual? What would be the advantages and disadvantages of your particular recruitment strategy?
2. How might genetic or biological explanations of sexual orientation be combined with social or learning explanations to more completely capture how sexual orientation likely develops for most individuals?
3. Suppose you encountered the following headline: "Researchers Discover the Lesbian Gene." What questions would you have if this were the only information you were given?

CASE FOR ANALYSIS

Suppose that researchers are interested in the possible role that childhood teasing plays in the development of sexual orientation. They secure a grant to fund a large-scale study in which respondents are interviewed regarding their sexual orientation and are asked to recall instances in which they were teased over issues related to gender and sexuality. To generate a sample of heterosexual respondents, the researchers place an advertisement in several newspapers asking for volunteers for a study of "childhood experiences." The ad explains that participation involves a brief telephone interview for which respondents will be sent a check for $10 as compensation for their time. To ensure an adequately large sample of gay, lesbian, and bisexual individuals, the researchers place the same advertisement in several publications targeted to gay, lesbian, and bisexual readers. In an attempt to address the potential problems with categorizing individuals as to their sexual orientation, researchers only include in their sample those individuals whose self-identified sexual orientation matches their reported sexual experience. Those individuals who indicate a discrepancy between self-labeling and sexual experience are dropped from the sample. The researchers discover that childhood teasing over sexuality and gender issues was reported much more frequently among individuals in their nonheterosexual sample than in their heterosexual sample. The researchers conclude that childhood teasing may play an important role in the development of a sexual orientation that does not conform to societal prescriptions.

PUBLISHED REPORTS FOR FURTHER PRACTICE

Bailey, J. M., Pillard, R. C., Neale, M. C., & Agyei, Y. (1993). Heritable factors influence sexual orientation in women. *Archives of General Psychiatry, 50*, 217–223.

Bogaert, A. F. (1998). Birth order and sibling sex ratio in homosexual and heterosexual non-white men. *Archives of Sexual Behavior, 27*, 467–473.

Hamer, D. H., Hu, S., Magnuson, V. L., Hu, N., & Pattatucci, A. M. L. (1993). A linkage between DNA markers on the X-chromosome and male sexual orientation. *Science, 261*, 321–327.

Kitzinger, C., & Wilkinson, S. (1995). Transitions from heterosexuality to lesbianism: The discursive production of lesbian identities. *Developmental Psychology, 31*, 95–104.

Meyer-Bahlburg, H. F. L., Ehrhardt, A. A., Rosen, L. R., Gruen, R. S., Veridiano, N. P., Vann, F. H., & Neuwalder, H. F. (1995). Prenatal estrogens and the development of homosexual orientation. *Developmental Psychology, 31*, 12–21.

Rosario, M., Meyer-Bahlburg, H. F. L., Hunter, J., Exner, T. M., Gwadz, M., & Keller, A. M. (1996). The psychosexual development of urban lesbian, gay, and bisexual youths. *The Journal of Sex Research, 33*, 113–126.

Rosenbluth, S. (1997). Is sexual orientation a matter of choice? *Psychology of Women Quarterly, 21*, 595–610.

Stokes, J. P., Damon, W., & McKirnan, D. J. (1997). Predictors of movement toward homosexuality: A longitudinal study of bisexual men. *The Journal of Sex Research, 34*, 304–312.

EDUCATION: ARE SEX EDUCATION PROGRAMS IN SCHOOLS EFFECTIVE?

11

Sex education in the schools has existed since the early 1900s (Kyman, 1998), and it continues today despite mixed results of research on the effectiveness of such programs (see Kirby & Coyle, 1997; and Grunseit, Kippax, Aggleton, Baldo, & Slutkin, 1997, for reviews). School-based sex education, though widespread, also remains a controversial and hotly debated issue (Hazard & Einstein, 1993). Why? Perhaps the answer has to do with peoples' differing viewpoints regarding what constitutes effective sex education (what should be the goal of sex education?). Without conducting solid empirical research on the issue, arguments will continue to be mired in personal opinion and idiosyncratic beliefs. However, to draw sound conclusions from such research, particular issues need to be addressed and certain critical questions answered adequately.

WAS THE RESEARCH DESIGN ADEQUATE OR APPROPRIATE FOR THE RESEARCH QUESTION?

Because the primary research question has to do with the *effects* of sex education, only an experimental design is adequate to address this issue. In many cases, conducting an experiment is not difficult because the researchers have control over to whom sex education is offered. For a true experiment, students in particular schools would be randomly assigned to two groups: one receiving sex education (an intervention group) and the other not (a control group). To demonstrate an effect of the sex education program, the students in the intervention group should demonstrate greater improvement with regard to certain outcome criteria compared to the students in the control group. If different sex education programs were being compared, then students could be randomly assigned to as many different groups as there are programs (plus perhaps a control group). Even in what seems like a simple scenario, however, there are important issues to consider (Dynarski, 1997; Kisker & Brown, 1997).

First, what if the researchers do not have control over assignment to intervention versus control groups (Kisker & Brown, 1997), perhaps because all students in a particular school district automatically participate in a sex education program? In this case researchers may try to generate a control group by comparing the students who received the sex education to similar students in a different school district who did not receive sex education. However, because the researchers did not control assignment to the conditions, the resulting study is quasi-experimental in nature. So, even if there are differences between the two groups, researchers are left unsure whether the apparent change in sexual functioning was due to the sex education or to some other variable(s) on which the two groups of students may have differed.

Because the research participants were not randomly assigned to groups, there may have been differences between the two groups from the start that would explain why the intervention group ended up with different levels of sexual knowledge, attitudes, or behavior. For example, in this scenario the students in the control group (from a different school district) might have been better off (or worse off) than the intervention group with regard to initial sexual knowledge, or the two groups might have differed with regard to initial sexual attitudes and behavior. Compared to the students in the control group, the students in the intervention group might have been from homes with parents who were better or less educated, wealthier or poorer, and so forth. These possible differences between the two groups of students might explain any differences between them with regard to changes in sexual knowledge, attitudes, and behavior.

Another important question is what constitutes an adequate control group? Researchers could use the same group of students for both a control and intervention group by monitoring the students' sexual knowledge, attitudes, and behavior prior to and after participation in a sex education program. In a sense, the students are serving as their own control group. The problem is that without another distinct comparison group, who is monitored over the same time period as the sex education program but who did not participate in it, any changes over time might be due to factors other than the educational program. For example, particular events in the larger culture or in the mass media may occur at the same time as the sex education program, such as a widely watched television program or movie having to do with sexual topics or a celebrity who is announced to have AIDS. These cultural or media events may have an influence on students' sexual knowledge, attitudes, and behavior.

From a methodological standpoint, ideally individual students within a school system would be randomly assigned to either participate or not in the sex education program (Dynaski, 1997; Kisker & Brown, 1997). In real life, however, this is typically impractical if not impossible. Instead, classes of students are typically assigned to either group. If classes are not randomly assigned, a potential dilemma is whether students who take certain classes (or who have different teachers) differ systematically from students who take other types of classes. The ultimate issue is whether each student in the school system has an equal chance of being included in the intervention group or the control group. Suppose, for instance, that a sex education program is offered during a time slot allotted for elective courses. Researchers (or school administrators) then decide to assign students in metal shop, woodworking, and mechanics classes to receive the sex education program, and students in cooking, home management, and psychology classes will serve as the control group. Might the students who take these types of courses differ in substantial ways to begin with? How? Might such differences be related to initial sexual knowledge, attitudes, and behavior, or the effect sex education may have on the students?

There are also several potential problems having to do with administering sex education programs in a standardized fashion. That is, even though there is liable to be a written curriculum and also perhaps certain printed and video materials shown to students, in the end the sex education program is administered by a person (or people). Typically sex education programs, because they constitute only a small portion of the larger curriculum for a school year, are conducted by teachers whose primary roles involve teaching standard subjects such as social science or biology. The extent of training such teachers receive for handling sensitive material such as that involved in sex education is an important issue, as is the personal comfort level and attitudes of the teacher (de Gaston, Jensen, Weed, & Tanas, 1994). If he or she holds negative attitudes toward sexuality, or is unsure or uncomfortable with the material, this is sure to be apparent to students (and may affect the students' views toward the program and how much they receive from it). Any effects of a sex education program (or lack of effects) may have as much or more to do with the teachers than the actual program itself.

WHO WERE THE PARTICIPANTS?

Up to this point the discussion has focused on ways in which the sample might not be representative of all students in a school system because of selection factors introduced by the researchers or the school administrators. There are also instances in which *self-selection bias* might be a potential concern (Cohen, Byrne, Hay, & Schmuck, 1996). Because sex education is still a somewhat controversial issue, in some schools parental consent is required prior to participating in the program. In other cases, parents are requested to be involved in the program (e.g., Weeks et al., 1997). If this is the case, how might families in which parents refuse to be involved or to allow their children to be exposed to sex education differ from families who provide such involvement or permission? Might such background variables be related to initial sexual knowledge, attitudes, and behavior, as well as how the students might respond to the educational material?

In the case of parental consent and participation, technically the term *self-selection bias* does not fit, as it is not necessarily the students themselves who are selecting whether to participate. However, regardless of whether parental involvement or consent is required for participation in a sex education program, some students are not included (or at least not as much) simply due to their missing school. If the students who miss sex education classes differ systematically from those students who attend regularly, then the results obtained in a study of the effects of a sex education program may not generalize to all students. What types of students are most likely to miss school? Might they differ in their sexual attitudes and behavior compared to students who attend school consistently?

A similar issue is involved in self-reported variables the researchers may be using as evaluation criteria. If the effects of a sex education program are measured by responses to self-administered questionnaires, students always have the option of leaving some or all of the items blank. If students who tend to do so differ from those who answer questions consistently, a potential form of bias (and lack of generalizability) are introduced into the study. Unfortunately there are other potential problems with self-reports as they pertain to evaluation of sex education programs.

WHAT WERE THE QUESTIONS OR MEASURES USED IN THE RESEARCH?

Although there may be some consensus as to whether sex education should be offered in schools (McKay, Pietrusiak, & Holowaty, 1998), there is great debate about what such programs should include. Accordingly, what are considered outcome variables, or desirable effects of the program, may vary largely across studies. How should researchers evaluate whether a sex education program was successful or effective? Many people might agree that an effective program should positively affect students' behavior. However, just as with sexuality research generally, there is heavy reliance on self-reports when researchers evaluate the effects of sex education, and such self-reports entail inherent limitations and concerns (Sonenstein, 1997).

One potential problem with measuring self-reported effects of an intervention has to do with participants' expectations. Previous research has demonstrated that, when people believe they have participated in an intervention that should affect their behavior, they tend to report such improvements in their behavior, even if there has not been any such improvement (Dawes, 1988). One explanation of this phenomenon is that people often do not remember precisely what their behaviors (or attitudes) were like prior to the intervention, so it is possible to recall that things were worse than they were because of the assumption that the intervention must have had some positive effect. So, when people participate in a sex education program, they may report (and honestly believe) there has been at least some improvement in their behavior, regardless of whether the intervention was effective. For example, this self-perceived improvement may involve reports that the participants now use condoms with greater consistency than before the sex education program.

The tendency for students to overreport positive changes in their attitudes and behavior might particularly be a problem when the students know they are participating in a study of the effects of sex education. In this case, not only are there expectancy effects, but respondents might feel some pressure not to let the researchers or teachers down by being a program failure (or a bad student or research participant). Through their involvement in the sex education program, students are made aware of what the "correct" attitudes and behaviors are (because those are the ones promoted in the program), even if these do not match their actual attitudes and behaviors. So, after exposure to sex education, respondents may have a relatively better sense for what the researchers consider to be desirable responses to sexual questions. One could say that sex education may be as much or more about teaching the "appropriate" answers to questions about sexual attitudes and behavior as it is about actually changing those attitudes and behaviors. Researchers may be more likely to elicit such "correct" (but inaccurate) responses from students if questionnaires are completed in school where students may feel that anonymity and confidentiality are not guaranteed.

Because self-reported changes in attitudes and behavior are suspect, ideally researchers would measure some more objective outcome variable (Sonenstein, 1997). Researchers do not have direct access to information about students' sexual behavior and attitudes, so such objective measures must be based on public information regarding the effects or consequences of students' attitudes and behavior. For example, if students are actually more likely to abstain from sexual intercourse or to use condoms after having participated in a sex education program, then there should be a subsequent decline in rates of sexually transmitted disease and unwanted pregnancy among those students. If there are particular clinics where the students are able to seek treatment and advice for these concerns, then researchers can monitor whether the total numbers of cases handled in the clinics decrease after termination of the sex education program. Of course there are substantial problems with such measures: the clinics may serve many other patients who were not students in the sex education program, students who were participants in the program may seek treatment elsewhere, and so forth.

WHAT DO THE RESEARCH RESULTS MEAN?

Given the potential problems with adequate control groups, selection biases, and self-report biases, it is important to carefully interpret the results of research on the efficacy of sex education interventions. Many of these problems lead to questionable generalizability. So, one question to ask is, Are the results these researchers obtained liable to apply to students in general? If not, is there anything the results might reveal about effective sex education with certain types of students? What types of interventions might be more effective with what types of students?

With regard to outcome measures, were they all based on self-report? If so, how much did students' self-reports accurately reflect their sexual attitudes and behavior, rather than a result of students providing answers that were expected of them? If the outcome measures include some that are not based on self-reports, are the findings with those variables similar to the findings based on self-reports? If not, which set of findings seems more credible? Why?

Another question in interpreting results has to do with size of the effect. Is the effect associated with sex education large enough to be of practical value? Because research on sex education often involves large samples of students, small effects or differences are liable to be statistically significant. Recall that *significant* in this sense is a statistical concept and may have little to do with the size of the effect of the program (see Chapter 5). The difference in sexual attitudes and behavior between an intervention group and control group may be statistically significant yet may not be large enough to make a real difference in the lives of participants. This might be particularly true when the outcome measures are based on self-reports, which may tend to overrepresent the degree of improvement. Undoubtedly, sex education is beneficial for many students. Attempting to study its efficacy, however, is a difficult task fraught with many potential pitfalls.

QUESTIONS FOR DISCUSSION

1. To help resolve the ongoing debate over whether sexuality education should be offered in schools, how might you go about performing research to address the issue of what people believe should be the outcomes of an effective program? How might you go about determining what people in general believe should be the goals of sexuality education in schools?
2. Can you think of ways to attempt to measure the effects of sexuality education programs in schools that would *not* rely on self-reports from the student participants? What would be the advantages and disadvantages?

3. Suppose you encountered the headline, "School Administrators Declare Sex Ed a Success." What questions would you have if this were the only information available to you?

CASE FOR ANALYSIS

Suppose researchers wish to investigate the effects of a school-based program designed to promote sexual abstinence among high-school students. The researchers do not have control over administration of the program, so they locate a high school in which the program had been administered to 11th graders for the previous three years. For comparison purposes they choose a comparable high school in a neighboring county in which no form of sexuality education has been offered. The researchers then administer anonymous questionnaires to students in the senior class, asking each whether he or she has ever engaged in sexual intercourse, whether condoms were used in the most recent experience of sexual intercourse, whether the student has ever contracted a sexually transmitted disease, has had an unwanted pregnancy, and so forth. The administrators at the first school are not pleased when the researchers find a lack of differences in the rates of reported sexual and related experiences between the two samples. A local newspaper runs an article on the findings and includes the headline, "Local Sex Ed Program a Bust!"

PUBLISHED REPORTS FOR FURTHER PRACTICE

Arnold, E. M., Smith, T. E., Harrison, D. F., & Springer, D. W. (1999). The effects of an abstinence-based sex education program on middle school students' knowledge and beliefs. *Research on Social Work Practice, 9*, 10–24.

Buysse, A., & Van Oost, P. (1997). Impact of a school-based prevention programme on traditional and egalitarian adolescents' safer sex intentions. *Journal of Adolescence, 20*, 177–188.

Eisenman, R. (1994). Conservative sexual values: Effects of an abstinence program on student attitudes. *Journal of Sex Education and Therapy, 20*, 75–78.

Kassirer, A., & Griffiths, J. (1997). The effectiveness of "The Responsible Sexuality Program": A brief high school sexual education intervention. *Journal of Sex Education and Therapy, 22*, 5–11.

King, B. M., Parisi, L. S., O'Dwyer, K. R. (1993). College sexuality education promotes future discussions about sexuality between former students and their children. *Journal of Sex Education and Therapy, 19*, 285–293.

Kirby, D., Korpi, M., Adivi, C., & Weissman, J. (1997). An impact evaluation of project SNAPP: An AIDS and pregnancy prevention middle school program. *AIDS Education and Prevention, 9* (Suppl. A), 44–61.

Siegel, D., DiClemente, R., Durbin, M., Krasnovsky, F., & Saliba, P. (1995). Change in junior high school students' AIDS-related knowledge, misconceptions, attitudes and HIV-preventive behaviors: Effects of a school-based intervention. *AIDS Education and Prevention, 7,* 534–543.

Weeks, K., Levy, S. R., Gordon, A. K., Handler, A., Perhats, C., & Flay, B. R. (1997). Does parental involvement make a difference? The impact of parent interactive activities on students in a school-based AIDS prevention program. *AIDS Education and Prevention, 9* (Suppl. A), 90–106.

CHILD SEXUAL ABUSE: IS SEXUAL CONTACT BETWEEN A CHILD AND AN ADULT HARMFUL?

CHAPTER

12

The title of this chapter may seem ridiculous. How can child-adult sexual contact, or child sexual abuse, *not* be harmful? Some people may hold very strong beliefs about the answer to the question; preconceived beliefs about the effects of child-adult sexual contact are widespread, even coloring the way the issue is presented in college textbooks on sexuality (Rind, 1995). Considering logically the question of the effects of child sexual abuse is difficult because the issue includes some questions that are only implied, such as what constitutes child sexual abuse, what types of harm are involved, and how common and long-lasting are any harmful effects? Numerous studies have been conducted attempting to address the effects of child sexual abuse, and many times the results vary from study to study (see Fergusson, 1999; Kendall-Tackett, Williams, & Finkelhor, 1993; Polusny & Follette, 1995; and Rind, Tromovitch, & Bauserman, 1998, for reviews). This chapter will examine why this might be the case.

WAS THE RESEARCH DESIGN ADEQUATE OR APPROPRIATE FOR THE RESEARCH QUESTION?

In this case, because causality is the issue (the effects caused by child sexual abuse), the most definitive type of study would be an experiment. If a researcher took a group of children and randomly assigned them to either a sexual abuse group or a control group (where the children were monitored over time but nothing was done to them), then any resulting differences between the two groups could be attributed to the sexual abuse experienced by the first group. Obviously an experiment of this nature is inhumane and unethical and thereby impossible to conduct. So, what do sexual abuse researchers do instead?

90

The typical study on the effects of child sexual abuse compares a group of children or adults who experienced some type of child sexual abuse to a similar group of children or adults who were not abused (Briere, 1992; Pope, 1997). To the extent that the abused group displays more negative symptoms, such as depression or sexual dysfunction, the researchers speculate that the sexual abuse may have caused the difference between the two groups. However, the researchers are simply correlating abuse with symptoms, so issues of causality can be difficult or impossible to disentangle.

Assuming for a moment that child sexual abuse and some symptom, such as depression, are causally related, even the direction of causation is not always clear. Certainly it makes sense that experiencing child sexual abuse might lead to depression (Weiss, Longhurst, & Mazure, 1999). However, it also is possible that being prone to depression (or having low self-esteem that is related to depression) may make a child more vulnerable to adults looking for children to abuse. That is, certain characteristics of the child (e.g., low self-esteem, shyness, depression) may lead to a greater risk of a child being sexually abused, and these same characteristics may lead the individual to be at risk for certain negative mental health symptoms (Bailey & Shriver, 1999; Briere, 1992; Pope, 1997), and even negative sexual experiences (Gidycz, Hanson, & Layman, 1995; Messman & Long, 1996; Urquiza & Goodlin-Jones, 1994), later in life.

Previous research has indicated that when people are depressed they are more likely to recall negative childhood experiences compared to when people are not depressed (Lewinsohn & Rosenbaum, 1987). So, it is also possible that being depressed at the present time leads individuals to be more likely to remember or focus on child sexual abuse that did occur, or more likely to label certain sexual experiences during childhood as having been abusive (Briere, 1992; Pope, 1997). This may be particularly the case if the individuals being studied happen to live in a culture that supports the belief that child sexual abuse leads to depression.

Suppose that an individual watches television programs, reads books and magazines, and talks with a therapist, all of which say, in one form or another, that child sexual abuse causes depression (or other forms of harm). Suppose also that this person is having emotional difficulties and is confused as to why. In searching for a reason for the current problems, the person may be more likely to focus on some memory of inappropriate sexual experiences during childhood that the individual may now consider as having been abusive. Some researchers have found that, among women with depression, those who were sexually abused as children reported being more severely depressed than did the women who had not experienced abuse, although the two groups did not differ in the severity of depression as rated by psychiatrists (Gladstone, Parker, Wilhelm, Mitchell, & Austin, 1999). It may be that beliefs about the effects of childhood sexual abuse led to perceptions of having greater difficulties, at least among some women.

Because of certain issues involved in self-report, finding a correlation between self-reported childhood sexual abuse and current symptoms or problems in a questionnaire study may be the result of respondents drawing associations between these two things at the time when they are completing the questionnaire. Council (1993) examined the issue of context effects in questionnaire studies. He noted that when respondents are asked to complete a series of self-report measures in the same session, those that are completed first may have an impact on how respondents answer subsequent questions. In the case of childhood sexual abuse, respondents who report having had abusive experiences during childhood may be more likely to report current problems or symptoms because they are expected to follow, or because recalling experiences of abuse prompts the respondent to recall or focus on other problems in his or her life. To test this possibility, Council (1993) had college students complete measures of childhood sexual abuse and current psychological and emotional symptoms. However, half of the students completed the sexual abuse questionnaire first, whereas the other half answered the sexual abuse questions *after* having completed the measures of current symptoms. Childhood sexual abuse was correlated with current symptoms only in the condition when students completed the abuse questionnaire first.

Another problem with trying to determine causality from correlational studies involves the possibility that there is some third variable (or set of variables) that is related to the two variables being correlated, which therefore explains their correlation. In the case of child sexual abuse, perhaps some third variable, such as family dysfunction and having parents with significant emotional problems, makes children vulnerable to both sexual abuse and other negative experiences. That is, it is reasonable to expect that children who experienced sexual abuse may have been more likely to come from dysfunctional families and hence might also have been at much greater risk for other forms of maltreatment, such as inconsistent parenting, emotional abuse, physical abuse, and neglect. Having been raised in a problematic family and having experienced these other forms of maltreatment may cause, or at least contribute to, adult symptoms such as depression, sexual dysfunction, unstable relationships, and so forth (Gladstone et al., 1999; Moeller, Bachman, & Moeller, 1993; Wind & Silvern, 1992). If researchers measured *only* child sexual abuse and a current symptom, their study may reveal a correlation between the two, yet the contribution of other negative experiences to the symptom would go unrecognized.

Because it is impossible to perform an experiment, the next best methodological approach would involve a longitudinal research design. Instead of simply measuring both experience of child sexual abuse and emotional symptoms at one point in time, researchers could measure mental health and other variables in the same individuals at various points over the respondents' lifetime. If researchers started with a large sample of children, some of the children will

not have been abused up to the point of entering into the study, but will experience some form of sexual abuse subsequently. It would then be possible to
examine changes in these children over time (pre- and post-abuse). More negative changes in these children's well-being compared to the health of the children in the study who did not experience abuse would provide suggestive evidence for harmful effects of child sexual abuse.

Unfortunately, however, such a longitudinal design would not allow
researchers to rule out a third variable (e.g., family dysfunction) that might be
responsible for both the sexual abuse and negative outcomes. Also, because it
would be unethical for the researchers to allow the abuse to continue, or to
allow the abuse that had occurred to go unnoticed, it would be possible that
the children in the study who did experience sexual abuse at some point would
be treated very differently by the other adults in his or her life (once those
adults learned of the abuse). Because members of our culture typically believe
that child-adult sexual contact is harmful for the child, adults who learn that a
child has had such experiences might expect the child to have difficulties.
These adults may then arrange for the child to receive some type of treatment.
The expectations and messages that these concerned adults communicate
might lead the child to conclude that he or she was harmed by the sexual
contact.

Despite the potential problems with longitudinal research, child sexual
abuse researchers have recognized the value of longitudinal studies relative to
cross-sectional ones (Briere, 1992; Gidycz et al., 1995; Pope, 1997), but such
studies are costly in terms of time and other resources and require very large
samples when examining experiences such as child sexual abuse that occur to
a small minority of people. An imperfect solution is to measure third variables
that may be responsible for observed correlations between sexual abuse and
symptoms and then statistically control for those third variables. In essence,
the researcher is asking, "After statistically accounting for the relationship
between the third variables and the symptoms, does knowing whether the
individual experienced sexual abuse add anything to the ability to predict
whether the individual is experiencing symptoms?" If the answer turns out to
be "no," we are still left unsure whether the sexual abuse or the third variables
were the more prominent cause of the symptoms (or perhaps the primary
cause is due to still other variables related to the third variables the
researchers measured). However, a "no" answer at least raises the *possibility*
that the third variables the researchers measured, and not the sexual abuse per
se, were the primary or unique cause of the symptoms.

Rind, Tromovitch, and Bauserman (1998) took just such a statistical
approach by examining correlations between child-adult sexual contact and
current emotional and mental functioning among college students. A unique
aspect of their research was that they performed statistical analyses on the
findings of all of the studies they could find relating childhood sexual abuse

with current psychological adjustment among college student samples (59 such studies in all). In this way Rind and his colleagues were not relying on simply one sample or a particular measure of child sexual abuse or psychological adjustment. Their findings caused a good deal of controversy, partly because the relationship between child-adult sexual contact and current functioning was small within college student samples. A more controversial aspect of their research was their conclusion that, once they statistically controlled for family functioning, the small relationship between child sexual abuse and current functioning all but disappeared.

Rind and his colleagues concluded that the *family functioning* of college students, which was related to students' experience of child sexual abuse, was a better predictor of whether the college students had emotional problems than was the occurrence of sexual abuse per se. Once they accounted for the family background of the college students, knowing whether students also had been sexually abused did not help predict which students were having mental health problems (also see Brock, Mintz, & Good, 1997). It seems that when child sexual abuse is linked with subsequent problems in the victim's functioning, it may be because that individual had multiple negative experiences in childhood, of which sexual abuse was one part. The combination of negative factors in childhood may lie behind subsequent problems, rather than a simple one-to-one correspondence between child sexual abuse and later symptoms. Of course Rind and his colleagues based their conclusions on college student samples only (but see Rind & Tromovitch, 1997, for similar analyses on results from national samples). An important issue in any research on the effects of child-adult sexual contact is how well the results generalize to other groups of people.

WHO WERE THE PARTICIPANTS?

When examining possible links between child sexual abuse and subsequent symptoms, it is important to consider who is being studied (Fergusson, 1999; Pope, 1997). Researchers are typically interested in possible negative consequences of child-adult sexual contact that are of an emotional or mental health nature. So, studying samples of individuals who are almost sure to either have such problems or not have such problems may bias the findings. For example, if researchers studied individuals who sought counseling or other psychiatric services, the researchers would be sure to find individuals with significant emotional and mental health problems. In fact, perhaps the large majority of such individuals would have substantial problems; otherwise why would they be motivated to seek treatment? The extent to which these problems are the result of child-adult sexual contact would be difficult, if not impossible, to determine.

In contrast, suppose that researchers studied samples that are almost sure to contain relatively few individuals with significant mental health concerns, such as high-achieving young adults (i.e., college students). Now the bias may run in the other direction in that researchers may be less likely to find an association between child sexual abuse and current emotional and mental health. The issue in both extremes has to do with a restriction in range. That is, in each type of sample there is a relatively narrow range of the mental health spectrum that one would find in the larger community. So, possible relationships between child sexual abuse and current emotional and mental functioning will not be as clear, and findings may not generalize to the larger population of individuals who have experienced child sexual abuse.

The issue of who is being studied also pertains when the researchers are comparing a group of individuals who have been abused to a similar group who has not experienced abuse. Earlier the point was brought up about how there may be a third set of variables that explains the apparent link between child sexual abuse and current symptoms. If the two groups differ with regard to these third variables, it may be misleading to conclude that the difference in emotional and mental health between the two groups is due to the fact that they differ with regard to abuse history.

To take an extreme example, suppose that researchers compare a group of women who are undergoing counseling and who have indicated to their therapist that they experienced child sexual abuse to a group of college student women who are enrolled in psychology classes and who, in a survey, denied having experienced child sexual abuse. The two groups do indeed differ with regard to self-reported history of abuse, but they are also liable to differ with regard to age, socioeconomic status, educational status of their parents, intelligence, family background, and so forth. To find that the sexually abused women indicate more symptoms would not be surprising given that they were sampled from a mental health treatment setting, whereas the nonabused women were sampled from a nonmental health setting.

So, what about only sampling women who are undergoing counseling and comparing those who have been abused to those who have not? These two groups are likely to be more similar than those in the previous example. However, the family functioning, likelihood of other forms of abuse, and still other variables are liable to differ between the two groups of counseling clients. Any difference between the two groups with regard to symptoms may be a result of these other differences, or at least a combination of child sexual abuse and these other variables.

In attempting to answer the question of whether child-adult sexual contact causes harm, the ideal appears to be sampling individuals from the general community (Rind & Tromovitch, 1997). Researchers would want to recruit people in such a way that nearly everyone had an equal chance of being selected for participation. However, because potential respondents cannot be made to participate, researchers always end up with less than 100% cooperation. The issue then becomes whether the people who agree to participate differ from the nonvolunteers with regard to important variables.

In the case of child sexual abuse, it is important to ask how potential respondents were recruited. Imagine that potential respondents were first approached, whether by telephone, mailed survey, or interviewer, to participate in "a study examining the effects of child sexual abuse." Who might be most likely to agree to participate? Those people who were abused or those who were not? Those people whose abuse was particularly damaging or those for whom their child-adult sexual experience seems a relatively minor event in their past? The answers to these questions may be unknown, but if one group is more likely than another group to participate, the results may not be representative of the general population.

WHAT WERE THE QUESTIONS OR MEASURES USED IN THE RESEARCH?

So far we have been talking about child sexual abuse as though it is a definite experience that everyone would recognize. In reality, however, definitions of what constitutes child sexual abuse vary across individuals, including mental health professionals who deal with abused individuals on a regular basis (Berliner & Conte, 1993; Haugaard, 1996; Heiman, Leiblum, Esquilin, & Pallitto, 1998). Researchers also are not immune from individual variation, so even the definitions of child sexual abuse used by researchers have varied considerably (Rind & Bauserman, 1993; Rind & Tromovitch, 1997; Roosa, Reyes, Reinholtz, & Angelini, 1998).

Child sexual abuse might be defined as any contact with a child's genitals for the sexual pleasure of the adult, or it might be defined to include exposure of an adult's genitals to a child. Still, do genitals even have to be involved for an act to qualify as child sexual abuse? What about fondling a child's buttocks, or showing a child sexually-explicit photographs or videos, or talking to a child in a sexually seductive manner? To determine whether an act constitutes child sexual abuse, does it matter whether the child experiences the interaction positively or negatively? Does there have to be coercion, force, or physical trauma associated with the sexual contact? Does it matter what the nature of the relationship is between the child and adult, such as a stranger or a family member? Does the age of the child matter in determining whether an experience is a case of child sexual abuse?

These are difficult questions with which researchers must grapple when studying child sexual abuse. Because there has been a great deal of variation in researchers' decisions regarding these and other definition issues, the results of studies have also varied widely, despite the fact that the focus of all such research has been child sexual abuse (Roosa et al., 1998). Consider two hypothetical examples: The first team of researchers defines child sexual abuse as any sexual interaction between a child under the age of 16 years and an individual who is at least five years older than the child. Sexual interaction in this case includes kissing, fondling, or being exposed to sexually-explicit images, as well as genital stimulation or penetration of the child's body. The second team of researchers defines child sexual abuse as any physical contact between an adult at least 18 years of age and a child 12 years of age or younger, involving force, where the genitals of one or both of the individuals were stimulated for sexual pleasure or the child was penetrated anally. Can you imagine how each team of researchers might uncover different rates of child sexual abuse within even the same sample? Which team do you think would be most likely to discover a relationship between the experience of child sexual abuse and negative experiences linked to the abuse?

One potential problem with a very broad definition of child sexual abuse is that some individuals who had such experiences will not consider them to have been abusive. Previous research indicates that child sexual play and curiosity may be fairly common (Lamb & Coakley, 1993; Okami, Olmstead, & Abramson, 1997), so when responding to the first team of researchers mentioned above, it is possible to envision a research participant who, at age 10, had a 15-year-old neighbor one day share his stash of sexually explicit magazines with the respondent. This respondent would be classified as having had an experience that the researchers consider child sexual abuse, yet the respondent may not consider it to have been abusive. To avoid this problem, why not just ask people, Have you ever experienced child sexual abuse? Here we would be leaving it up to the individual to decide whether he or she had ever experienced an incident that he or she now considers to have been abusive.

Asking respondents to make a determination as to whether their experience constituted child sexual abuse seems to solve some definition problems. However, it almost guarantees that the researchers will find a relationship (correlation) between child sexual abuse and negative experiences such as depression, emotional distress, or problems in coping. This would be the case because the word *abuse* implies trauma and harm, so people who had child-adult sexual experiences that they found traumatic or harmful would be most likely to indicate that their experience was an instance of abuse. Indeed, it appears that people who believe their childhood sexual abuse experiences to be severe or traumatic may be most likely to experience current mental health problems (Williams, 1993).

Beyond definition issues, does the wording of the questions regarding child sexual abuse have an effect on how willing people might be to disclose or admit to having had such experiences? In Western culture, child sexual abuse is considered a very negative experience at best and an unspeakable, heinous crime at worst. Individuals who were victims of child sexual abuse might feel stigmatized by the experience, and they may experience fear that admitting having been abused would lead others to see them negatively (e.g., as "damaged goods," or at least partially to blame for what happened). So, what incentive would research participants have to disclose child sexual abuse, particularly in face-to-face interviews with a stranger?

Another potential problem with asking people about child sexual abuse involves the fact that researchers are asking respondents to recall something that may have happened to them many years ago, possibly at a very young age (Fergusson, 1999; Pope, 1997). How accurate are our memories regarding events that occurred to us as young children? How accurate are our memories regarding events that occurred to us many years ago? One might argue that the experience of child sexual abuse, particularly if defined as involving force or trauma, would be an event sure to stand out in a persons's memory. However, this may not necessarily be the case (Loftus, Garry, & Feldman, 1994; Loftus & Pickrell, 1995), particularly if people have the ability to mentally repress memories of traumatic events as a way to cope with them (Chu, Frey, Ganzel, & Matthews, 1999; Williams, 1994). On the other hand, repressed memories may not exist, yet the belief that such memories are possible may lead some individuals to construct such "memories" and falsely recall having experienced childhood sexual abuse (Lief & Fetkewicz, 1995; Loftus & Ketcham, 1994).

Recalling the timing of child-adult sexual contact may be difficult, making questions about child sexual abuse that contain a time qualifier (e.g., abuse that occurred prior to age 10) potentially problematic. The issue, of course, involves the concept of time, and it appears that memory does not contain an aspect of remembered time per se. That is, people use different methods for trying to locate a remembered event in time, and these methods may be prone to distortion, particularly as the event becomes more distant in time (Friedman, 1993). Overall, one should be leery of results based on asking people about events that occurred several years ago or when the individuals were very young, regardless of the nature of the events (Henry, Moffitt, Caspi, Langley, & Silva, 1994).

WHAT DO THE RESEARCH RESULTS MEAN?

As can be seen from the issues raised in this chapter, such seemingly simple questions as, What proportion of people have been sexually abused as children? and Does child sexual abuse cause harm? can be difficult if not impossible to answer with a high degree of confidence. When researchers perform a single study and make a strong knowledge claim based on their findings, chances are they are taking too simplistic an approach to understanding what is likely a complex issue. Some of the reasons for the ambiguity in findings across studies include relatively narrow samples, varied ways of defining and asking about child sexual abuse, varied ways of defining harm (including whether the effects being considered are short-term or long-term), and failing to consider possible third variables that might explain apparent correlations between child sexual abuse and problems later in life.

When encountering knowledge claims regarding child sexual abuse, it is important to be sensitive to the ways concepts were defined, respondents were sampled, and the questions were asked. For example, how might gender factor into the equation? People may be more likely to label an experience of child-adult sexual contact as sexual abuse if the child was relatively young and the adult was the same gender as the child compared to incidents involving relatively older children and adults of the other gender (Maynard & Wiederman, 1997). Also, males who experienced sexual contact with an adult while they were children may be less likely than females with similar experiences to consider those experiences as abusive or to indicate that the experiences caused any harm (Holmes, Offen, & Waller, 1997; Laumann, Gagnon, Michael, & Michaels; 1994; Rind et al., 1998), and even the effects of child sexual abuse may be different for males compared to females (Weiss et al., 1999). So, people who encounter a headline or statement in a textbook that declares "One third of Americans were sexually abused as children," should ask how child sexual abuse was defined, what were the exact questions respondents answered, and who were the research participants, including the proportion who were male compared to female.

When faced with knowledge claims regarding the effects of child-adult sexual contact, it is important to examine whether the research design (as well as the measures and participants) warrants the conclusions the researchers drew. Because a causal link between child sexual abuse and subsequent negative effects seems so intuitive, it is easy to slip into inferring causality based on simple associations. For example, Weiss et al. (1999) reviewed the previous research literature on relationships between child sexual abuse and adult depression. They concluded that "There is considerable evidence that childhood sexual abuse has long-term effects" (p. 825). However, all of the research they reviewed was correlational in nature.

If the research was sound, and the conclusions drawn are appropriate given the limitations of the research, then one should ask how strong the relationships are. There may be a statistically significant relationship between having experienced adult-child sexual contact and subsequent harm, but perhaps substantial negative effects apply to only a relatively small portion of the individuals who had such childhood experiences. This would not detract from the seriousness of the issue, nor would it minimize the trauma those individuals experienced. However, if a minority of individuals who experienced

adult-child sexual contact appear to have negative effects, it would be inaccurate to imply that such childhood events invariably cause the child harm (Pope, 1997; Rind et al., 1998).

QUESTIONS FOR DISCUSSION

1. The results of some research discussed in this chapter suggest that it may be family dysfunction in general, rather than child sexual abuse specifically, that results in problems in adulthood for those who were sexually abused as children. Theoretically, then, children in perfectly healthy families who happened to experience child-adult sexual contact should display little if any harm. Do such cases seem plausible? Why or why not?
2. If you were conducting research in this area, what definition of sexual abuse would you use? What is your rationale? What are advantages and disadvantages of your definition?
3. Suppose you encountered a magazine article with the headline, "Ten Signs of Child Sexual Abuse." The article describes signs that parents or others might use to determine whether there is reason to be concerned that a particular child has been sexually abused. What questions would you have about the article and the advice it communicates?

CASE FOR ANALYSIS

Suppose researchers are interested in the possible effects of child-adult sexual contact shortly after such contact occurs; however, researchers only have access to college student research participants. Questionnaires are distributed to students at the end of class in a variety of courses, and those who decide to participate are asked to return the anonymous questionnaires to the next class meeting (and to place them in a box containing other completed questionnaires).

In the questionnaire the students are asked to recall "any instances during childhood in which an adult acted in a sexually inappropriate way with you." Students are also asked to describe the nature of any such event or events that they remember and to complete a checklist regarding the "immediate effects" the experience had on the respondent. Students are instructed to place an X next to any or all of the items in the checklist that describe how the sexually inappropriate experiences affected the respondent as a child. The many items in the checklist included "felt ashamed," "lost trust in adults," and "suddenly began having nightmares." The researchers find that the large majority of respondents who indicated having experienced child sexual abuse also indicate having experienced multiple negative effects immediately following the abuse.

PUBLISHED REPORTS FOR FURTHER PRACTICE

Bartoi, M. G., & Kinder, B. N. (1998). Effects of child and adult sexual abuse on adult sexuality. *Journal of Sex & Marital Therapy, 24,* 75–90.

Bensley, L. S., Van Eenwyk, J., Spieker, S. J., & Schoder, J. (1999). Self-reported abuse history and adolescent problem behaviors. I. Antisocial and suicidal behaviors. *Journal of Adolescent Health, 24,* 163–172.

Duane, E. A., Stewart, C. S., & Bridgeland, W. M. (1997). Consequences of childhood sexual abuse for college students. *Journal of College Student Development, 38,* 13–23.

Feiring, C., Taska, L., & Lewis, M. (1999). Age and gender differences in children's and adolescents' adaptation to sexual abuse. *Child Abuse & Neglect, 23,* 115–128.

Kenny, J. W., Reinholtz, C., & Angelini, P. J. (1997). Ethnic differences in childhood and adolescent sexual abuse and teenage pregnancy. *Journal of Adolescent Health, 21,* 3–10.

Luster, T., & Small, S. A. (1997). Sexual abuse history and number of sex partners among female adolescents. *Family Planning Perspectives, 29,* 204–211.

Wiederman, M. W., Sansone, R. A., & Sansone, L. A. (1998). Disordered eating and perceptions of childhood abuse among women in a primary care setting. *Psychology of Women Quarterly, 22,* 493–497.

Wiederman, M. W., Sansone, R. A., & Sansone, L. A. (1999). Bodily self-harm and its relationship to childhood abuse among women in a primary care setting. *Violence Against Women, 5,* 155-163.

THERAPY AND DYSFUNCTION: HOW WELL DOES SEX THERAPY WORK?

The rates of sexual problems or sexual dysfunction in the United States may be surprisingly high (Laumann, Paik, & Rosen, 1999; Spector & Carey, 1990). Over the last few decades, several approaches to treatment and counseling for sexual problems have been developed (Wiederman, 1998). How does one know whether these treatments, often lumped together under the term *sex therapy*, are effective in alleviating sexual problems and dysfunction? Are some approaches or techniques more effective than others? These are the types of questions researchers attempt to answer when studying the effects of sex therapy. When conducting methodologically sound research on psychological interventions, whether it be counseling, psychotherapy, or sex therapy, there are several potentially problematic issues that need to be addressed.

WAS THE RESEARCH DESIGN ADEQUATE OR APPROPRIATE FOR THE RESEARCH QUESTION?

Because the primary research question has to do with the effects of sex therapy, only an experimental design is adequate to address the issue of cause and effect. Conducting an experiment may be possible in this case because the researchers are often in control of whether sex therapy is administered. For a true experiment, people interested in receiving sex therapy would be randomly assigned to two groups: one receiving sex therapy (a treatment group) and the other not (a control group). To demonstrate efficacy of the therapy, the participants in the treatment group should demonstrate greater improvement than the participants in the control group. If different forms of sex therapy were being compared, then potential patients could be randomly assigned to as many different groups as there are treatments (plus perhaps a control group). Even in what seems like a simple scenario, however, there are important issues to consider.

102

For one, what if the researchers do not have control over assignment to therapy, perhaps because all clients contacting a treatment center are automatically assigned to some form of therapy? These researchers may try to generate a control group by contacting people in the community who report that they too need sex therapy but have not received it. The researchers might then try to compare degree of sexual functioning in the treatment and control groups after a specified length of time in therapy. However, because the researchers did not control assignment to the conditions, the resulting study is quasi-experimental in nature. So, even if there are differences between the two groups (presumably the treatment group would report better sexual functioning after treatment, whereas the control group would not report improved functioning), the researchers are left unsure whether the apparent change in sexual functioning was due to therapy or to some other variable(s).

Because the research participants were not randomly assigned to groups, there may have been differences between the two groups from the start that would explain why the treatment group ended up with better sexual functioning. For example, in this scenario the control group may have been less motivated to improve their sexual functioning; the lower level of motivation may have been demonstrated by the fact that they did not seek out treatment, whereas the people in the treatment group did. The participants in the control group might have been better off (or worse off) than the treatment group with regard to initial sexual dysfunction. Compared to the people in the control group, the participants in the treatment group might have been better educated, wealthier, younger or older, and so forth. These possible differences between the two groups might explain any differences between them with regard to improvement in sexual functioning.

Another important question is what constitutes an adequate control group? People who want therapy but who are told there will be a delay before therapy can begin are often referred to as *waiting list controls*. These individuals will eventually receive treatment, but while they are waiting for therapy their sexual functioning is studied for comparison to the group receiving treatment. If people seeking sex therapy are randomly assigned to treatment or the waiting list, then the researchers assume that the two groups are equivalent with regard to background variables (e.g., age, motivation, degree of sexual dysfunction), so any differences between the two groups after the one group receives treatment is presumed to be due to the sex therapy. However, the two groups differ in one important way: one group knows they are receiving treatment, whereas the other is still waiting for the desired therapy.

Researchers long ago recognized that peoples' expectations can drastically influence their experience. So, people involved in sex therapy probably have greater expectations for improvement in their sexual functioning compared to people who are still on a waiting list to begin treatment. Regardless of how effective the treatment actually is, the expectation that it will help may result in improvement in sexual functioning for at least some people. Researchers refer to this phenomenon as a *placebo effect* (Critelli & Neumann, 1984; Horvath, 1988). The notion is that people can be given a placebo, a "treatment" that actually should not have any effect, and people's functioning may improve because the participants *believe* that the treatment should have some effect. So, the sex therapy group may demonstrate improvement relative to the waiting list control group, but such differences may be due to placebo effects rather than the effect of therapy.

To counter placebo effects, researchers sometimes use a bogus treatment (placebo) as a control group (Quitkin, 1999). In this way the members of both the treatment and control groups share the expectation that their sexual functioning should improve. However, an adequate placebo control group must be believable to participants; they must believe that they are receiving legitimate treatment. Because sex therapy typically involves counseling people, listening patiently and empathically to their problems in a nonjudgmental manner (Wiederman, 1998), constructing a placebo control group that does not share some of these characteristics is difficult if not impossible. A placebo control group for sex therapy might involve participants meeting weekly with a "therapist" who simply listens to the participants describe and discuss their sexual difficulties. Would any improvement in this group simply be due to expectations of improvement, or might simply having a nonjudgmental professional listen have some beneficial effects, at least for some patients? Research has consistently demonstrated that disclosing emotional experiences results in improved mental and physical health (Pennebaker, 1997), so simply sharing with a "therapist" one's experience of having problems in sexual functioning is liable to have a beneficial effect, even though it may not be considered therapy by the researchers.

There are also several potential problems having to do with administering the sex therapy in a standardized fashion. That is, if three therapists are conducting the sex therapy in one study, how do the researchers know whether each is conducting therapy in similar ways? The researchers might require a prescribed format that each therapist has to follow, but then one might question the generalizability of results, since this form of sex therapy probably does not reflect what sex therapists would do on their own (if they were not part of a rigidly controlled research project) as they address the concerns of different types of clients.

A similar issue is involved in conducting a placebo control group. If the placebo treatments are implemented by different therapists than are the actual treatments, how do researchers know that any resulting differences between the patients in each group is not due to the fact that each saw different therapists? Perhaps the therapists in one condition were simply friendlier, or seemed more authoritative, or were more likable. In an attempt to control this problem, sometimes the same therapists are used to conduct both the actual and the placebo treatments. Still, each therapist knows the difference between the two conditions, and expectations the therapist holds regarding which treatment should work may have effects on the actual success with patients.

Because of these and other methodological issues, research on treatment efficacy is among the most difficult types of research to conduct. As there has been a relative lack of sound research on the efficacy of sex therapy in particular (Rosen & Leiblum, 1995; Wiederman, 1998), it is important to be especially critical when examining the methods that were used to evaluate the effects of sex therapy. One such methodological issue involves the research/treatment participants.

WHO WERE THE PARTICIPANTS?

By definition, participants in sex therapy research are individuals who report some degree of sexual difficulties, or dysfunction. Beyond this generalization, there are various ways participants in such research are recruited, and potential effects associated with each type. To take one historic example, Masters and Johnson (1970) reported the results of research on their then-innovative approach to the treatment of sexual dysfunction. Their success rates were extremely high and far exceeded the rates experienced by therapists who subsequently tried Masters and Johnson's techniques. Why did Masters and Johnson's (1970) research results not seem to generalize to other therapists?

One possible explanation has to do with the fact that the patients Masters and Johnson (1970) treated traveled to their clinic in St. Louis and agreed to participate in their intensive program. Sex therapy consisted of daily sessions, and the patients, while in St. Louis, focused on little except their treatment. So, the patients Masters and Johnson saw were liable to be highly committed, well-educated, and financially secure as they traveled from various parts of the country (at their own expense) to receive treatment. The types of patients sex therapists saw in their local offices may have been less likely to respond to treatment because of differences in background variables compared to Masters and Johnson's (1970) patients.

In contrast to research participants being more motivated than typical patients, there may be instances in which research results do not generalize to other patients because the research participants are lower in motivation. Such might be the case, for example, if researchers offer free treatment or financially compensate participants for their involvement in a study of sex therapy. In these cases some participants may be less motivated, involved in therapy, or may have less serious sexual dysfunction compared to real-life patients who seek out and pay for treatment.

Methods of advertisement may also limit the generalizability of research results. If free treatment is offered and potential participants are recruited through newspaper or radio advertisements, might these individuals differ in substantial ways from people who decide on their own to seek out treatment and then actually make the necessary arrangements? Regardless of ways in which participants in sex therapy research may differ from typical patients, they often also differ in that they are required to complete measures or answer specific questions regarding their sexual functioning. Research participation involves providing certain self-reports that are not typically required of patients in sex therapy. These self-reports are then used to determine whether the treatment was successful, so it is a good idea to examine closely how sexual functioning is assessed within each particular study.

WHAT WERE THE QUESTIONS OR MEASURES USED IN THE RESEARCH?

Rarely is sexual functioning, and possible improvement in such functioning, measured directly in research on the efficacy of sex therapy. Like all forms of sexuality research, there is heavy reliance on self-reports. Accordingly, there are specific measurement issues to consider in evaluating sex therapy research. For example, one issue, as noted earlier, is the potential problem of expectancy effects in producing improvements in sexual functioning apart from any true effects of treatment. A similar phenomenon is possible with self-reports.

Previous research has demonstrated that, when people believe they have participated in an intervention that should affect their performance, they tend to report such improvements in their performance, even if there has not been any such improvement (Dawes, 1988). One explanation of this phenomenon is that people often do not remember precisely what their functioning was like prior to the intervention, so it is possible to recall that things were worse than they were because of the assumption that the intervention must have had some positive effect. So, when people participate in sex therapy, they may report (and honestly believe) there has been at least some improvement, regardless of whether therapy was effective.

The tendency for people to overreport improvement in their sexual functioning might particularly be a problem when respondents know they are participating in a study of the effects of sex therapy. In these cases, not only are there expectancy effects, but respondents might feel some subtle pressure not to let the therapist or researchers down by being a treatment failure (or a "bad" patient or research participant). Similarly, they may experience some internal, self-imposed pressure not to see themselves as a failure, particularly if they were invested in therapy and had sought out and paid for treatment. These tendencies may work to bias their recall and self-report of how things have changed in the sexual aspects of their lives.

WHAT DO THE RESEARCH RESULTS MEAN?

Given the potential problems with adequate control groups, standardization of therapy, recruitment biases, and self-report biases, one should be careful in interpreting the results of research on the efficacy of sex therapy. Many of these problems lead to questionable generalizability. So, one important issue is, Are the results these researchers obtained liable to apply to sex therapy patients in general? If not, is there anything the results might reveal about effective sex therapy with other types of patients?

With regard to outcome measures, were they all based on self-report? If so, how likely is it that patients' self-reports accurately reflected changes in their sexual behavior, rather than a case of providing answers that were expected of them? If the outcome measures include some that are not based on self-reports, are the findings with those variables similar to the findings based on self-reports? If not, which set of findings seems more credible? Why?

Another question in interpreting results has to do with the size of the effect. Is the effect of sex therapy large enough to be of practical value? That is, the difference in sexual functioning between a treatment group and control group may be statistically significant, yet may not be large enough to make a noticeable difference in the lives of participants. This might be particularly true when the outcome measures are based on self-reports, which may tend to overrepresent the degree of improvement. Undoubtedly, sex therapy is successful for many people (Rosen & Leiblum, 1995; Wiederman, 1998) and is a legitimate option for those experiencing sexual difficulties. Attempting to study its efficacy, however, is a very difficult task fraught with many potential pitfalls.

QUESTIONS FOR DISCUSSION

1. Suppose researchers are interested in examining the effectiveness of a particular treatment for low sexual desire. How might they go about measuring the possible effects of treatment on subsequent sexual desire? What potential problems might arise with such a measure?
2. Exactly what type of control group would you recommend for a study on the effectiveness of sex therapy? Precisely how would the conditions in

the control group be similar and different from the treatment group? What effects might these similarities and differences have on the results?

3. Suppose that you encounter an advertisement for treatment of sexual dysfunction that includes the statement that the clinic, or program, or treatment has been "successful in more than 90% of its cases." What questions would you have about this claim? What information would the people who made the claim have to provide to persuade you of their success rate?

CASE FOR ANALYSIS

Suppose researchers are interested in comparing two commonly performed types of treatment for problems with sexual arousal. To perform a fair test of how each form of treatment is conducted in the "real world," the researchers locate six therapists, three of whom perform each type of treatment and have done so for several years. The researchers attempt to recruit research participants by running advertisements in local newspapers and other publications, announcing that they are offering free treatment for difficulties with low sexual arousal. Potential participants call a toll-free telephone number where a member of the researchers' staff answers questions and gathers contact information for those callers who want to begin treatment. As callers indicate an interest in treatment, each is randomly assigned to one of the six therapists, who then conducts treatment as he or she typically would. Research assistants briefly interview each research participant every four weeks regarding current sexual functioning and improvement in the ability to get sexually aroused when the individual so desires. These data are then analyzed to determine whether one type of treatment is more effective than the other, and whether one type of treatment results in quicker improvement.

PUBLISHED REPORTS FOR FURTHER PRACTICE

Gupta, M. (1999). An alternative, combined approach to the treatment of premature ejaculation in Asian men. *Sexual and Marital Therapy, 14,* 71–76.

MacPhee, D., Johnson, S. M., & Van Der Veer, M. M. C. (1995). Low sexual desire in women: The effects of marital therapy. *Journal of Sex & Marital Therapy, 21,* 159–182.

Ochs, E. P. P., & Binik, Y. M. (1998). A sex-expert computer system helps couples learn more about their sexual relationship. *Journal of Sex Education and Therapy, 23,* 145–155.

Ravart, M., Trudel, G., Marchand, A., Turgeon, L., & Aubin, S. (1996). Efficacy of a cognitive-behavioural treatment model for hypoactive sexual desire disorders: An outcome study. *Canadian Journal of Human Sexuality, 5,* 279–293.

Sarwer, D. B., & Durlak, J. A. (1997). A field trial of the effectiveness of behavioral treatment for sexual dysfunctions. *Journal of Sex & Marital Therapy, 23,* 87–97.

Stravynski, A., Gaudette, G., & Lesage, A. (1997). The treatment of sexually dysfunctional men without partners. A controlled study of three behavioural group approaches. *British Journal of Psychiatry, 170,* 339–344.

Wylie, K. R. (1997). Treatment outcome of brief couple therapy in psychogenic male erectile disorder. *Archives of Sexual Behavior, 26,* 527–545.

PORNOGRAPHY: IS VIEWING SEXUALLY EXPLICIT MEDIA HARMFUL?

Contemporary Western culture is saturated with sexually explicit media (SEM) of varying degrees of explicitness. On one end of the spectrum, images of scantily clad models in sexually suggestive poses are commonplace in advertisements. At the other end, people have relatively easy access to videotapes, magazines, and Internet sites containing depictions of just about every type of sexual activity imaginable. The pervasiveness of SEM begs the question, Does exposure to SEM cause harm? This is a socially relevant question, and, although it continues to be hotly debated, it is difficult to answer with empirical research (Allen, D'Alessio, & Brezgel, 1995; Davis & Bauserman, 1993; Russell, 1998). The focus of this chapter is discussion of some of the potential pitfalls when conducting research on the effects of SEM.

WAS THE RESEARCH DESIGN ADEQUATE OR APPROPRIATE FOR THE RESEARCH QUESTION?

If researchers are interested in the effects of SEM, an experiment is most appropriate. Participants would be randomly assigned to one of two conditions: one is exposed to SEM (the experimental group), and the other is not (the control group). Assuming that the two groups differ only with regard to exposure to SEM, any subsequent differences between the two groups would be attributed to the first group having been exposed.

If the two groups differed in any way other than exposure to SEM, researchers would be left unsure whether any subsequent difference between the two groups is due to the initial difference. For example, participants in the control condition may spend an equal amount of time viewing nature scenes or popular movies without sexual content. If, immediately after exposure, participants who viewed SEM act differently than do participants in the control group, or if they report different attitudes, perhaps it is because they are still

110

in a state of relatively greater sexual arousal. In this case the experimental and control groups differ not only with regard to exposure to SEM but also with regard to level of sexual arousal. Perhaps the members of the control group would act similarly had they spent their laboratory time engaging in sexual fantasy or masturbation (without exposure to SEM).

Several experiments on the effects of SEM have been conducted (Allen et al., 1995; Davis & Bauserman, 1993), but the results do not necessarily answer the original question. To have the necessary control over conditions, researchers who conduct experiments on the effects of SEM must expose participants to SEM in the laboratory. Doing so calls into question the generalizability of findings: Does limited exposure to SEM in the laboratory mirror the experience of being exposed to SEM in the outside world?

The generalizability question in research on this topic is a persistent one because laboratory conditions are unlikely to re-create exposure to SEM as it is usually experienced. For example, exposure in the laboratory is generally limited to a single session, or perhaps a few sessions, whereas consumers of SEM in the outside world are liable to be exposed numerous times and for extended periods of time in each session. Note that this potential discrepancy between the outside world and the laboratory may effect generalizability in unknown ways. If laboratory research fails to reveal effects of exposure to SEM, one could still argue that real-world exposure does cause effects, because it is typically greater in frequency and duration than that used in the laboratory. However, if laboratory research did reveal effects of exposure to SEM, one could still argue that real-world exposure does not cause such effects, because the greater frequency and duration of such exposure desensitizes the individual to the material.

Another issue of generalizability has to do with the actual SEM used in research. Such material varies widely with regard to the sexual activities portrayed, the degree of violence or degradation included in the depictions, and so forth. Not all SEM is the same. So, what types should researchers study? Does the type of SEM researchers expose participants to reflect the type of SEM people expose themselves to in the outside world? If not, the findings of the research do not capture what occurs in typical cases. Even if samples of SEM used in research are representative of what many people consume in the real world, the samples are still limited to a very small slice of what is available to consumers, so it is always difficult to determine whether effects in the laboratory would generalize to everyday experience.

With regard to the content of SEM, perhaps it is specific types of content that lead to harm, and other types of SEM have no effect. For example, researchers have found that exposure to violent media (with no sexual content) may negatively affect attitudes and behavior (e.g., Paik & Comstock, 1994; Zillman & Weaver, 1999). If the SEM that researchers use contains violence, they may find an effect of exposure to the material. However, without a comparison condition in which SEM was used that did not contain violence, it would be unclear whether it was the sexual material or the violent material that had an effect on viewers.

Because of the problems of generalizability when conducting laboratory studies of the effects of SEM, some researchers study relationships between self-exposure to SEM and other variables. Their work is based on the assumption that if exposure to SEM has particular effects on certain attitudes and behavior, researchers should find a correlation between degree of exposure to SEM and those particular attitudes and behaviors (e.g., Frable, Johnson, & Kellman, 1997). Of course, finding such a correlation would not allow researchers to draw valid conclusions regarding causality. It may be that holding certain attitudes leads to seeking out SEM, rather than exposure to SEM causing those attitudes.

Another possibility is that exposure to SEM and particular attitudes and behaviors are correlated because of their relationship to some other variable (and not because exposure to SEM and attitudes and behaviors cause one another). For example, perhaps having a very strong interest in sexual stimuli and sexual activity causes certain individuals to seek out SEM, to engage in sexual activity with a relatively large number of partners, and to take a somewhat casual attitude toward having sex with a partner who was not well known to the individual. If researchers did not account for "sex drive" as a variable, they may be tempted to explain the correlation between exposure to SEM and number of sex partners as causal (i.e., "exposure to SEM leads to a casual orientation toward sex").

Some researchers examined potential effects of SEM by correlating amount of SEM with particular behaviors (such as number of rapes) at the societal level (Bauserman, 1996; Kimmel & Linders, 1996; Winick & Evans, 1996). The assumption behind their work is that if exposure to SEM causes particular behaviors, then one should find more of those behaviors in places where SEM is more prevalent, or an increase in those behaviors when SEM is suddenly more available in a particular place (Diamond, 1999; Diamond & Uchiyama, 1999). For example, if exposure to SEM leads to an increased propensity to rape, then the amount of SEM sold in particular cities, states, or countries should be positively related to the number of rapes in those places (Russell, 1998).

Compared to laboratory studies, this societal level of analysis removes concerns about generalizability. However, researchers have no control over the variables, so issues of causality remain uncertain. For example, suppose that researchers attempted to show that as the amount of SEM in a culture increased or decreased over time, so did the incidence of rape. Even if this were found to be the case, the amount of SEM and frequency of rape may have simultaneously varied because of other changes occurring in the culture at the same time, not because SEM and rape were causing one another. For example, perhaps there was a demographic shift in the proportion of men in the culture. Because men account for the large majority of consumers of SEM and perpetrators of rape, an increase in the number of men in a culture will tend to result in increases in SEM and rape. Also, correlations between variables at the societal level may not translate into similar correlations at the individual level. Last, researchers taking the societal-level approach are still faced with decisions regarding which types of SEM to correlate with what particular behaviors. For example, does one correlate the incidence of rape with the number of magazines sold or the number of videos produced? If so, which types of magazines or videos should be chosen for correlation?

WHO WERE THE PARTICIPANTS?

One potential issue regarding the generalizability of research results on the effects of SEM has to do with participants. Frequently, such research participants are either college students or convicted sex offenders (Bauserman, 1996; Davis & Bauserman, 1993). One could argue that college students have had less exposure to SEM than many adults in the larger community, whereas convicted sex offenders probably have had greater exposure than the norm. So, studying effects of exposure to SEM in these two groups may not represent the results one would find with general community members. Note that simply finding a high incidence of exposure to SEM among convicted sex offenders does not warrant evidence that such exposure leads to sexual offenses. First, one must compare the extent of exposure to SEM to that experienced by people in general to determine whether indeed it is greater among sex offenders. If it is, researchers still do not know whether SEM leads to sexual offenses, performing sexual offenses leads to an interest in SEM, or both variables are caused by some other variable such as personality disturbance or compulsive sexuality.

Even among college students or community members, however, those who participate in studies on the effects of SEM may differ substantially from members of the larger population. Research on volunteer bias has revealed that men are much more likely than women to volunteer for studies involving SEM, and regardless of gender, volunteers for such studies appear to be more liberal in their sexual attitudes and more sexually experienced compared to those who decline to participate (Plaud et al., 1999; Wiederman, 1999b). If potential research participants know in advance that participation involves exposure to SEM, researchers are liable to end up with a relatively select group of participants. Whether the research results generalize to people who refuse to participate in such studies is unknown, but it is worth considering.

WHAT WERE THE QUESTIONS OR MEASURES USED
IN THE RESEARCH?

Besides the fact that SEM can vary widely across studies, researchers differ in how they measure potential effects of exposure to it. Potential effects that are studied typically have to do with negative attitudes toward women and increased likelihood of acting aggressively toward women (Byers, 1988; Russell, 1998). In real-world settings, such potential effects might be demonstrated through hostile, callous remarks made about and toward women and through engaging in sexual harassment, coercion, or assault. These experiences are difficult to examine in a laboratory setting, yet researchers attempt to measure both attitudinal and behavioral effects of exposure to SEM.

What about simply asking participants to reveal effects SEM has had on their attitudes and experience? Some researchers have taken this approach (e.g., Gunthar, 1995). However, this methodology assumes that respondents have insight into how their attitudes and behavior have been affected, and that they are willing and able to report such effects. Typically researchers try to measure potential effects of exposure to SEM more directly. Still, to measure attitudes, researchers usually rely on self-reports. Respondents might be asked to complete a scale measuring attitudes toward women both prior to and after exposure to SEM in the laboratory.

Unfortunately, such self-reports are prone to intentional and unintentional distortion. For example, the research participants may figure out that the researcher is examining possible effects on their attitudes; why else would they be asked to complete the measures before and after exposure to SEM? Accordingly, some respondents might tend to indicate changes in their attitudes, either because they believe that SEM is harmful or because they figure that is what the researchers expect. Other respondents might be careful to respond very similarly both times because they do not view themselves as the type of person whose attitudes could so easily be swayed. Either way, the results in the laboratory may not reflect accurately what would occur should the same respondents have encountered the same SEM in the outside world.

Frequently researchers have attempted to avoid the problems with self-reports by unobtrusively observing how participants interact with women after having been exposed to SEM. In such experiments, participants are given a bogus reason for being exposed to SEM, such as being asked to rate how arousing the respondent finds each of several video clips. Immediately afterward, participants may be led to believe that, although their participation in the study is finished, there is another, supposedly unrelated study for which the researcher needs participants. That study typically includes an opportunity for the participant to act cruelly or callously toward a female who the participant believes is another research participant (but who in actuality is an assistant to the researcher). In many such studies the female may provoke or anger the participant, such as by providing negative feedback about the participant or expressing views opposite to those held by him. The variable the researchers are interested in is how the male participant will act toward the female peer.

In a similar researcher design, participants are led to believe that they have completed participation in the project. Then participants are simply observed in a casual setting, such as a room where they wait with others for the researcher to return and excuse them from the experiment. Somewhere in the casual setting appears a female confederate, again who may in some way provoke the male participant. The female may leave the setting, then the researchers either ask the participant what he thought of the female or they observe how the participant talks about the female to others who are present.

In both types of research designs, the researchers examine whether more hostility is expressed toward the female when research participants viewed SEM than when participants viewed nonsexual media. A critical question is whether such laboratory responses translate into how males might respond to females in the outside world after having viewed SEM. For example, encountering a female who provokes the participant in some way immediately after exposure to SEM, and having the opportunity to apply some form of punishment to that female, is liable to be rare in the outside world. However, when put into the situation in the laboratory, respondents may feel some pressure to act cruelly.

In one study, male research participants watched sexually explicit films, after which they had the opportunity to criticize or punish a female confederate who had evaluated the research participant negatively (Fisher & Grenier, 1994). The men had the option of providing verbal feedback to the woman over an intercom, administering shocks to her from a different room, or simply leaving the experiment. The option to simply leave the experimental setting had not been included in previous research. Virtually none of the men chose to administer shocks. Such a finding calls into question what the laboratory research results mean with regard to real-world behavior.

WHAT DO THE RESEARCH RESULTS MEAN?

Researchers examining potential effects of exposure to SEM have the choice between pursuing an experimental or correlational approach. So, one initial question researchers should ask in interpreting findings has to do with causality. The results of correlational studies do not allow for inferences as to causality. Although a true experiment theoretically allows for conclusions regarding cause and effect, there are controversial aspects to experiments on SEM. For example, was there a control group for comparison? Were participants randomly assigned to conditions? Were the experimental and control groups truly comparable except for exposure to SEM (including level of sexual arousal)? If not, then perhaps other variables (such as sexual arousal) explain the different results between the experimental and control groups.

Even within well-conducted experiments, there are numerous questions, the answers to which would influence how credible the results should be considered. For example, what type of SEM was used in the experiment? Who were the participants and how representative are they of the larger population? What do the researchers mean by "effects" of exposure to SEM, and how were such effects measured? Answers to these and similar questions help researchers determine how justified they are in drawing conclusions from their particular study to the effects of SEM on people in general.

There are other, perhaps more complex questions regarding the effects of SEM that researchers either have not yet tackled or are just beginning to examine. For example, if exposure to SEM has negative effects, are they long-lasting? How can such effects be remedied? Are certain types of individuals relatively prone to (or resistant to) negative effects of exposure to SEM (e.g., Byers, 1988)? If so, what characteristics are related to being easily influenced? These and other important questions remain for future investigation.

QUESTIONS FOR DISCUSSION

1. If you were to conduct an experimental study on the possible effects of exposure to SEM, how would you choose to go about locating and selecting actual SEM for use in the experiment? What are the advantages and disadvantages of your methods?
2. If researchers find a positive correlation between the amount of SEM sold across locations and the number of sex crimes in those places, one explanation might be that exposure to SEM increases the likelihood of acting sexually aggressive toward others. What are some alternative explanations? Typically there has been a negative correlation between the availability of SEM in a culture and the degree of sexual aggression in that culture (Diamond, 1999). What are some possible explanations?
3. Suppose you encounter the following headline: "Pornography Linked to Series of Rapes." The feature goes on to describe how a recently convicted rapist was found to have a large quantity of SEM of all types in his house. What questions would you have regarding the implication that the SEM was somehow related to the sexual aggression?

CASE FOR ANALYSIS

Suppose researchers interested in the possible effects of viewing violent pornography decide to conduct an experiment. First, they survey the local stores where sexually explicit videotapes are sold or rented to determine what are the most popular videos. From these the researchers select the tape they judge to be most violent. Because the tape they choose is approximately 90 minutes long and they do not have that much time with research participants, the researchers make a copy of the videotape, editing out all scenes that do not contain some form of violence (the resulting tape is about 30 minutes long).

The researchers recruit possible male participants through a college student participant pool. Because the policies at their particular university require that researchers inform potential participants at the point of sign-up what research participation involves, the sign-up sheets include the explanation that involvement in the research includes viewing a sexually explicit videotape. When research participants show up to the experiment, each is randomly assigned to either view the sexually violent videotape or to watch approximately 30 minutes of a sexually explicit videotape that was also among the most popular (but which does not contain violence). Participants view the tapes in groups of 5–10 students.

After viewing one of the videotapes each participant completes a questionnaire containing several items, including an item that asks the respondent to rate how likely he would be to force a female to have sex if he was sure that he would not be caught. This rating of likelihood is statistically significantly higher in the group who saw the violent videotape compared to the group who saw the nonviolent videotape. The researchers conclude that viewing SEM that contains violence may increase the likelihood of rape by men.

PUBLISHED REPORTS FOR FURTHER PRACTICE

Barak, A., & Fisher, W. A. (1997). Effects of interactive computer erotica on men's attitudes and behavior toward women: An experimental study. *Computers in Human Behavior, 13,* 353–369.

Bauserman, R. (1998). Egalitarian, sexist, and aggressive sexual materials: Attitude effects and viewer responses. *The Journal of Sex Research, 35,* 244–253.

Davies, K. A. (1997). Voluntary exposure to pornography and men's attitudes toward feminism and rape. *The Journal of Sex Research, 34,* 131–137.

Diamond, M., & Uchiyama, A (1999). Pornography, rape, and sex crimes in Japan. *International Journal of Law and Psychiatry, 22,* 1–22.

Frable, D. E. S., Johnson, A. E., & Kellman, H. (1997). Seeing masculine men, sexy women, and gender differences: Exposure to pornography and cognitive constructions of gender. *Journal of Personality, 65,* 311–355.

Jansma, L. L., Linz, D. G., Mulac, A., & Imrich, D. J. (1997). Men's interactions with women after viewing sexually explicit films: Does degradation make a difference? *Communication Monographs, 64,* 1–24.

Kimmel, M. S., & Linders, A. (1996). Does censorship make a difference? An aggregate empirical analysis of pornography and rape. *Journal of Psychology & Human Sexuality, 8*(3), 1–20.

Mullin, C., & Linz, D. (1995). Desensitization and resensitization to violence against women: Effects of exposure to sexually violent films on judgments of domestic violence victims. *Journal of Personality and Social Psychology, 69,* 449–459.

LOVE: WHAT IS THE ROLE OF LOVE IN SEXUAL INTERACTIONS?

CHAPTER

15

In contemporary Western culture people frequently link romantic love to sexual feelings and experiences (De Munck, 1998; Seidman, 1991). Indeed, there seems to be a great deal of overlap in the concepts "in love" and "sexual attraction" (Marston, Hecht, Manke, McDaniel, & Reeder, 1998; Myers & Berscheid, 1997; Regan, Kocan, & Whitlock, 1998). Accordingly, the majority of Americans claim that they would not have sexual relations with another person unless they were in love with that individual (Laumann et al., 1994). These findings imply that love is an important aspect of sexuality for many contemporary Americans. Still, there is the empirical question, To what extent does love explain the sexual decisions individuals actually make? Does love lead to sex, or sex lead to love, or both? Ultimately, the question posed here is, How do love for and sexual interactions with another person affect one another?

WAS THE RESEARCH DESIGN ADEQUATE OR APPROPRIATE FOR THE RESEARCH QUESTION?

Because the issue is one of effect, the most definitive type of study might be an experiment. Ideally a researcher would take a group of people, pair them up randomly with other individuals (strangers), and then randomly assign these couples to one of three groups. In the first group the couples would be made to fall in love with one another, in the second group the individuals would be made to engage in sexual activity together, and in the third group the couples would be made to interact socially (control group). As the experiment continues over the course of days, weeks, or months, the feelings and sexual activity of the couples would be monitored. If sexual interaction plays a particular role in fostering love, the couples in the second group should develop greater love for one another compared to the couples in the third group.

Likewise, if love plays a particular role in facilitating sexual interaction, sexual activity should be greater in the first group of couples compared to the couples in the third group.

Obviously an experiment of this nature is impossible to conduct. Because researchers cannot force people to fall in love, the first experimental group would not exist. There may be some individuals who would volunteer to be participants in the second group (requiring sexual contact with another research participant), but how representative would these individuals likely be of the general population of adults?

Even if researchers could iron out these problems, would the experimental conditions mirror what occurs in real life? In reality, people themselves select others with whom to interact socially based on the level of attraction and similarity between the two individuals. From this pool of social contacts, people tend to fall in love with particular individuals and to select particular individuals as sexual partners based on feelings that emerge. The development of loving feelings and the process of becoming a sexual couple occur over some span of time, and much more is going on in the developing relationship between the two individuals besides sex and love. These other factors could have a tremendous effect on feelings and sexual interactions within the couple, and sex and love could, in turn, affect each other as well as these other relationships factors.

If researchers wish to study the relationship between love and sexual activity, what strategy could they realistically pursue? Such researchers could take a longitudinal approach in which dating couples and sexual partners are monitored over time, ideally from the very start of their relationship. If love and sexual activity are measured at various points, the researchers could attempt to determine which preceded the other, and whether increases in one reliably led to increases in the other. However, because there are other factors involved that the researchers cannot control or perhaps even measure, this approach would not allow for determination of causality. For example, it appears that people's beliefs about how people come together for a romantic relationship affect how those individuals actually behave in the relationship (Baldwin, 1995; Knee, 1998), and people's initial views of their partner may actually affect the type of relationship that develops with that individual (Murray, Holmes, & Griffin, 1996). So, although a longitudinal approach might provide some suggestive evidence that sex and love affect each other, there is always the possibility that other factors are responsible for the apparent association.

Researchers could take a cross-sectional approach that would involve measuring love and sexual activity at one point in time across numerous couples who vary in both. The resulting correlation between love and sex would indicate the strength or degree of their relation, but would not allow for inferences as to causality. Feelings of love could affect increased sexual interest in one's partner, or increased sexual activity with one's partner might facilitate feelings of love, or love and sex could be correlated because both are related to some third variable or set of variables.

A variation on the cross-sectional approach would involve asking respondents to retrospectively rate their degree of love at various points in their relationship (e.g., Grote & Frieze, 1998; Sprecher, 1999) and to recall the degree of sexual activity at each of those points (Christopher & Cate, 1984, 1985). The researchers could then calculate correlations between love and sex for each of those points in an attempt to determine whether the relationship between the two experiences changes over time within couples. Of course, the findings in such a case would be suspect because people were not being monitored over time, but simply asked to recall or estimate how they felt and what they did at various points. It may be that people's memories of their relationship and partner are affected by their current feelings (Harvey, Flanary, & Morgan, 1986; McFarland & Ross, 1987) as well as the stories they have formed about their relationship (LaRossa, 1995; McGregor & Holmes, 1999; Plummer, 1995; Sternberg, 1995). Sprecher (1999) asked dating couples to recall their previous feelings of love and actually measured their degree of love at multiple points over a span of several years. She found that, although there was some correspondence between peoples' perceptions of change and actual change in their feelings over time, that correspondence was far less than perfect.

Regardless of the research design, the focus of research on love and sexuality is liable to be respondents who are dating or married couples. As with any research, issues of generalizability from a particular sample to the larger population are relevant. So, it is important to consider who the research participants are.

WHO WERE THE PARTICIPANTS?

Participants in research focused on love and sexuality are frequently college students or individuals who recently married (often identified by consulting public records regarding marriage licenses filed within a particular time frame). From these populations, dating or married individuals or couples are recruited for possible participation in a study. The methods of recruitment, and problems that are encountered along the way, could lead to a rather specific or narrow subsample of the larger population (Acitelli, 1997; de Jong Gierveld, 1995).

Suppose that individuals were invited by telephone or advertisement to participate in a study examining "love and sexuality among couples," or simply a study on "couples' relationships." Would some types of couples be less likely to agree to participate? In this case one can imagine that those couples who are having problems in their relationship, perhaps resulting in decreased love and sexual activity, might be reluctant to participate, either out of embarrassment or lack of interest in spending additional energy focused on issues concerning their troubled relationship. What if researchers sampled couples who had applied for a marriage license within the previous year? Levels of loving feelings can be expected to be relatively high among newlyweds. In both of these cases, the researchers are liable to end up with a relatively healthy sample of couples, those who are most likely to report high levels of love and satisfying sexual interactions. Similar speculation can be made about any recruitment method in which the potential participants know in advance that their romantic relationship will be the focus of the research questions.

Karney and his colleagues (1995) actually examined the differences that would result from recruiting couples through various means. They compared couples recruited through newspaper advertisements to couples recruited through accessing marriage license information and found that the couples who responded to the newspaper advertisements exhibited relatively greater marital conflict. They then examined just the group accessed through marriage licenses and compared the couples who agreed to participate in research to those who declined and found that volunteers were of relatively higher socioeconomic status. These results suggest that, regardless of the method of recruiting couples to participate in research, the final sample the researchers end up with is going to be at least somewhat different than the larger population of couples from which the participants were drawn.

What Were the Questions or Measures Used in the Research?

A primary issue in research on love involves how the concept is defined and measured. Certainly, people in contemporary Western culture make a clear distinction between love *for* someone and being *in* love with someone (Lamm, Wiesmann, & Keller, 1998; Myers & Berscheid, 1997; Regan, 1998). Researchers too have made such a distinction and have developed several self-report instruments designed to measure some conceptualization of romantic love (Davis et al., 1998). As with all social science research, the results can be strongly influenced by the particular measures investigators choose.

Because contemporary Western conceptualizations of love include a strong emphasis on erotic attraction, several scales designed to measure romantic love do so by asking about feelings of passion toward, and sexual interest in, the loved one (Regan, 1998). Indeed, some researchers see conceptual romantic love as emerging from the same physiological arousal that may explain sexual desire (e.g., Hatfield & Rapson, 1987). If researchers used measures of love that are based on an arousal or attraction definition of love, it would not be surprising to find a fairly strong correlation between scores on the love scale and the frequency of sexual activity between the couple.

Even attempting to measure love through verbal questions and answers could affect the knowledge of what love is. McClelland (1986) discussed how romantic love, which is based heavily on feelings, is often measured by researchers using direct verbal reports. However, feelings may not translate well into words, and requiring research respondents to answer verbally may result in descriptions of people's experience that do not accurately capture their actual feelings.

What about simply asking research participants whether they are "in love," or the degree to which they are in love with a particular partner? This approach would not force the researchers' definition of love onto the respondents' experiences, but it would then be unclear what each respondent meant by their respective rating of love. Although there may be some core features of romantic love that are recognized by a majority of people within a particular culture (Aron & Westbay, 1996), there may still be a good deal of variation in what constitutes love across individuals as well as within the same individuals across different relationships (Beall & Sternberg, 1995; Thompson & Borrello, 1992). Indeed, people even seem to vary in their style or approach to love within romantic relationships, and even members of a particular dating or married couple may differ with regard to such love styles (Morrow, Clark, & Brock, 1995).

Because the question is, To what extent do love and sexual activity influence each other, why not simply ask people how their feelings for their partners have been related to their sexual interactions with those partners? The problem is that doing so requires certain assumptions on the part of the researchers. First, this approach assumes that people have good insight into how their feelings and behaviors are linked, and the influence each has on the other. Second, the researchers would have to trust that the answers respondents provided reflect their actual experience, rather than distortions that occur over time with peoples' memories or their beliefs about how sex and love are related. The research participants live in a culture in which love and sex are viewed as belonging together—romantic love entails a strong erotic attraction to the loved one, and love is viewed by many as the only legitimate reason for engaging in sexual activity with a partner. So, one concern would be that if asked, "How was your decision to have sexual intercourse with your partner affected by your feelings of love?" respondents might be likely to indicate that love played a substantial role, because to realize and admit otherwise would imply that they violated cultural expectations and values that they themselves may hold.

WHAT DO THE RESEARCH RESULTS MEAN?

Depending on the research design, participants, and measures, the conclusions that can be drawn from any particular study on the relationship between love and sexual activity may vary considerably. For correlational studies using self-report measures, the most appropriate conclusion may simply be that there is a relationship between peoples' *self-reported* love for their partner and having a sexual relationship together. Because of the concerns discussed above, one cannot necessarily conclude that love and sex affect one another—they may be related in a correlational study simply because respondents *believe* that they are related, so their answers to research questions may reflect those beliefs.

Perhaps love and sex are correlated because both are related to some third variable or set of variables (e.g., trust or comfort with the partner). Whether these third variables are conceptualized as part of love or separate from it will depend on the definition and measures of love the researchers choose. If love and sex are found to be related, there is the issue of the magnitude or size of the relationship. Are there other variables that may be even more important than love in understanding what motivates individuals and couples to engage in sexual activity?

With regard to the results, do they apply to people generally, or only to a specific type of individual or couple? As noted at the start of this chapter, people in contemporary Western culture generally view love as a primary motive for sexual activity with a partner. However, gender may moderate that relationship between sex and love such that the relationship between these two variables is stronger among women than among men (Taris & Semin, 1997). If researchers examine relationships between sex and love and do not consider potential differences between male and female respondents, the results may not generalize equally well to men and women. Similarly, if the research participants were college student couples, the results with that sample may not be the same as among people who are dating and of the same age but not college students (or who are married or older).

In summary, as savvy consumers of research, our role is to ask, What research design was used? Who were the research participants? How were love and sex defined and measured? And finally, are the conclusions the researchers drew appropriate given the answers to these questions?

QUESTIONS FOR DISCUSSION

1. If you conducted a study on love in sexual relationships, how would you define and measure *love*? What are the advantages and disadvantages associated with your choice?

2. Researchers could ask people directly what role such factors as love play in their decision to engage in sexual interactions with a particular person. What disadvantages might there be in pursuing this strategy?

3. Suppose you encountered the following headline: "Love Less Important for Sex Among Young Adults." The feature goes on to describe how a recently conducted national survey with respondents ages 18 years and older contained the question, "Have you ever had sex with someone whom you did not love?" The highest percentage of people responding "yes" were among the 21-to 25-year-old participants. What questions would you have about this research? Do you think the headline accurately summarizes the findings? Why or why not?

CASE FOR ANALYSIS

Suppose researchers are interested in the extent to which people's feelings of love for their partner are linked to sexual activity with that partner. In an attempt to address this issue, the researchers construct a very brief questionnaire that they distribute to people waiting in a large airport in their city. Respondents complete the questionnaire anonymously and return the completed questionnaire by placing it in a box that contains other completed questionnaires. The primary items of interest are a rating the respondent performs as to the degree of love they feel toward their current partner or mate, as well as an estimate of the number of times the individual engaged in sexual intercourse with their partner during the previous month. The researchers find a statistically significant positive correlation, such that those respondents who reported the most love for the partner generally report the most frequent sexual activity. However, the correlation was rather small and the researchers notice differences depending on the age of the respondents. The correlation between love and sexual activity is strongest among the youngest adults in the sample, whereas among the oldest age groups the correlation is extremely small and statistically nonsignificant (despite having a large sample). The researchers conclude that, despite any stereotypes to the contrary, love is less important as a prerequisite for sexual activity among older adults than among more recent generations.

PUBLISHED REPORTS FOR FURTHER PRACTICE

Cate, R. M., Long, E., Angera, J. J., & Draper, K. K. (1993). Sexual intercourse and relationship development. *Family Relations, 42*, 158–164.

Frey, K., & Hojjat, M. (1998). Are love styles related to sexual styles? *The Journal of Sex Research, 35*, 265–271.

Hendrick, C., & Hendrick, S. S. (1991). Dimensions of love: A sociobiological interpretation. *Journal of Social and Clinical Psychology, 10,* 206–230.

O'Sullivan, L. F., & Gaines, M. E. (1998). Decision-making in college students' heterosexual dating relationships: Ambivalence about engaging in sexual activity. *Journal of Social and Personal Relationships, 15,* 347–363.

Regan, P. C. (1997). The impact of male sexual request style on perceptions of sexual interaction: The mediational role of beliefs about female sexual desire. *Basic and Applied Social Psychology, 19,* 519–532.

Stephan, C. W., & Bachman, G. F. (1999). What's sex got to do with it? Attachment, love schemas, and sexuality. *Personal Relationships, 6* 111–123.

Taris, T. W., & Semin, G. R. (1997). Gender as a moderator of the effects of the love motive and relational context on sexual experience. *Archives of Sexual Behavior, 26,* 159–180.

Appendix

EVALUATING SEXUALITY INFORMATION POSTED ON THE INTERNET

As the World Wide Web continues to expand, it becomes an increasingly useful and enticing source of information. Accessing sexuality information via the Internet is quick and convenient, and the range of possibilities is vast. At the same time, however, information posted on the Internet is unregulated, and it is possible for virtually anyone to offer material that may be more or less accurate and useful. The critical-thinking skills you developed throughout this book will serve you well as you evaluate sexuality information on the World Wide Web. Still, there are a few specific questions you should ask to help assess the knowledge claims you encounter via the Internet. Each of these questions, which follow, involve related issues for you to consider.

IS THE SOURCE OF THE INFORMATION CREDIBLE?

Because posting knowledge claims on the World Wide Web does not require any formal education or scientific training, and such material does not have to undergo any form of peer review (as described in Chapter 1), the first goal should be to determine who is offering the information. Is the author or source of the Web site clearly identified? Is there a link to the home page for the organization that provided or sponsored the pages you are viewing? Is there at least enough information provided so that readers could contact the individual or institution who created the material to verify credibility? If the answer to any of these questions is "no," there is evidence for concern as to credibility of the source.

Is the site provided or sponsored by a reputable organization, or is the site someone's home page? In general, one should be more skeptical of information provided by individuals, regardless of their organizational affiliation or credentials, as opposed to official information provided by a respected government agency (e.g., the Centers for Disease Control), an educational institution (e.g., the University of Kansas School of Medicine), or a professional association (e.g., the American Psychiatric Association). This is not to say that information from any source is infallible, but some sources of information are likely to be more credible than others. The expectation is that knowledge claims provided by a recognized and respected institution have a greater likelihood of being objective and accurate than those posted by an individual. Much of the sexuality information posted on the Internet comes from individuals. The task for readers is to assess the credentials of these individuals. Is the author of the Web site qualified to make the claims he or she makes? Remember that holding an advanced educational degree (such as a doctorate) or a title (such as Director) does not necessarily make a person an unbiased expert on any particular topic.

Occasionally, Web site authors will create impressive titles for themselves, or equally impressive institutional names, to lend credibility to their material. Some of these institutions exist in name only. By creating institutions with phony, yet authentic-sounding, names, the author is trying to persuade readers that the material presented is legitimate and worth believing. Of course, individuals searching the Web for information may not recognize the name of any particular institution, even if that organization is well-established and reputable. Unfortunately, some individual Web sites are clever in their deception and have created names and layouts similar to those of well-known institutions. The point is simply to be skeptical of organizations that are not recognizable and to look for indications that the organization or institution is legitimate.

One way to tell if a Web site is legitimate is if it provides a description of the organization and its purpose, as well as complete contact information. One indication that the site is not a reputable source of information is if it seems to have an over-concern with presenting its credibility, such as focusing on the credentials of the author(s). Many times the authors of such Web sites are out to sell something, whether it is an opinion or a product. This point is examined closer in the next question of the discussion.

What Is the Purpose or Objective of the Material?

Some Web sites clearly intend to accurately inform readers about a particular sexuality topic, or perhaps to entertain through humor or parody. Many others appear to exist for the purpose of persuading the reader. In the area of sexuality, these sites may advocate a certain opinion (e.g., homosexuality or abortion is morally wrong) or advertise or sell products or services (e.g., books, counseling, sexual aids).

To obtain accurate information on the Internet, it is important to determine the objective of a Web site. When the underlying goal is to persuade readers of something, the information should be presented objectively, with any conflicting information also provided. Many people too easily assume that the most convincing argument is made when all of the material is in favor of the argued position, and any information that contradicts or does not support the argument is ignored, or perhaps discredited. This strategy may make for a strong argument, but it does not allow the reader to make a completely informed decision.

Rarely will a Web site explicitly state its purpose, so readers typically have to infer its purpose from the material presented. The source of the material, as mentioned earlier, is the first clue as to the Web site's purpose. Another clue may be found in the style in which the information is presented. Information from reputable institutions and researchers typically is presented in a way that is unemotional, that emphasizes sound logic, and does not offer absolutes, such as guarantees. When the goal of a Web site is to persuade, it is more likely to appeal to emotions (such as fear or anger), to use inflammatory language, and to present information in absolute terms, implying or stating that it is unquestionably correct.

Another possible clue as to the purpose of a Web site is whether there is an advertisement, or if a request is made of the reader to send a check or provide a credit card number. Advertising may be used to financially support legitimate Web sites that offer unbiased and accurate sexuality information. However, the question to ask is whether there appears to be a conflict of interest between the informational material and the advertisements that coexist on the same site. For example, if the Web site provides information on recently developed treatments for sexual dysfunction, and the advertisements on that site are not directly related to treatments for sexual dysfunction (e.g., links to sites for telephone long-distance providers or on-line bookstores), then there is little conflict of interest. In contrast, if that same site contains advertisements for books, therapists, or devices related to the treatments described in the information, then there is a conflict of interest, and readers should be skeptical about the objectivity of the information. In this last example, the purpose of the information (which may be presented as though it is a research report or a news story) may simply be to persuade the reader that the products for sale are worth buying.

WHAT IS THE OVERALL QUALITY OF THE INFORMATION PROVIDED?

Determining the quality of information posted on the Internet can be difficult. If people were experts on the topics they seek out, there would be no reason to turn to the World Wide Web for that information. Typically, people seek information to learn about a topic that is at least somewhat unfamiliar to them. Considering the credibility of the Web site, as well as the probable objective or goal of the site, will help determine how much weight to give to the information found there.

There are other issues to consider to get a sense of the quality of information. For example, how do the knowledge claims fit with what one already knows about the topic? Is it clear where the information presented in the Web site originally came from? Is the material on the Web site taken from an edited or peer-reviewed source? Can stated facts be verified through footnotes, bibliographies, or references provided? If statistics are provided, is it clear where they came from or how they were generated? How credible are those sources that are cited? Is the information timely? Are there indications of when the information was posted to the Internet, whether there have been attempts to update the material, and whether the information is the latest version? If links to other pages or other sites are provided, have those other pages or sites been maintained?

In addition to the more formal indicators of accuracy, such as references to sources, there are some informal things to look for that may raise suspicions as to the general quality of the material at a Web site. For example, are there obvious mistakes or lapses in logic in the material? What about the general quality of the writing? If there are obvious problems with grammar, spelling, and punctuation, or some of the written material just does not seem to make sense, one may question whether the author was equally careless or incompetent in gathering and evaluating the information posted on the Web site.

If information is presented graphically, are the depictions misleading in any way? Does it appear that graphs were included as a dramatic way to sway the reader or as a logical way to clearly present certain data? Does the author's argument rely on visual evidence, such as photographs, presented on the Web site? If so, it is important to remember that digital images are easily manipulated and that the old phrase "seeing is believing" is not always true.

Evaluating information posted on the Internet is not an exact science. You can improve your ability to find legitimate information, however, by consciously asking particular questions (such as those raised above) and applying your critical-thinking skills to various Web sites. Greater exposure to Internet sources of information makes answering the questions raised above easier.

In the end, there may not be clear indicators as to the credibility, purpose, or quality of a particular Web site. When in doubt, perhaps it is best to follow the path of the conscientious researcher who, when evaluating research that seems important, controversial, or not what one would expect, calls for replication of the information from other sources before accepting or acting on that information.

References

Acitelli, L. K. (1997). Sampling couples to understand them: Mixing the theoretical with the practical. *Journal of Social and Personal Relationships, 14,* 243–261.

Agnew, C. R., & Loving, T. J. (1998). The role of social desirability in self-reported condom use attitudes and intentions. *AIDS and Behavior, 2,* 229–239.

Agocha, V. B., & Cooper, M. L. (1999). Risk perceptions and safer-sex intentions: Does a partner's physical attractiveness undermine the use of risk-relevant information. *Personality and Social Psychology Bulletin, 25,* 746–759.

Allen, M., D'Alessio, D., & Brezgel, K. (1995). Summarizing the effect of pornography using meta-analysis: Aggression after exposure. *Human Communication Research, 22,* 258–283.

Anderson, P. B., & Aymami, R. (1993). Reports of female initiation of sexual contact: Male and female differences. *Archives of Sexual Behavior, 22,* 335–343.

Aron, A., & Westbay, L. (1996). Dimensions of the prototype of love. *Journal of Personality and Social Psychology, 70,* 535–551.

Atwood, J. D., & Siefer, M. (1997). Extramarital affairs and constructed meanings: A social constructionist therapeutic approach. *Journal of Sex & Marital Therapy, 23,* 55–75.

Bailey, J. M., Dunne, M. P., & Martin, N. G. (2000). Genetic and environmental influences on sexual orientation in an Australian twin sample. *Journal of Personality and Social Psychology, 78,* in press.

Bailey, M. J., Nothnagel, J., & Wolfe, M. (1995). Retrospective measured individual differences in childhood sex-typed behavior among gay men: Correspondence between self- and maternal reports. *Archives of Sexual Behavior, 24,* 613–622.

Bailey, J. M., & Pillard, R. C. (1995). Genetics of human sexual orientation. *Annual Review of Sex Research, 6,* 126–150.

Bailey, J. M., & Shriver, A. (1999). Does childhood sexual abuse cause borderline personality disorder? *Journal of Sex & Marital Therapy, 25,* 45–57.

Bailey, J. M., & Zucker, K. J. (1995). Childhood sex-typed behavior and sexual orientation: A conceptual analysis and quantitative review. *Developmental Psychology, 31,* 43–55.

Baldwin, J. D., & Baldwin, J. I. (1997). Gender differences in sexual interest. *Archives of Sexual Behavior, 26,* 181–210.

Baldwin, M. W. (1992). Relational schemas and the processing of social information. *Psychological Bulletin, 112*, 461–484.

Baldwin, M. W. (1995). Relational schemas and cognition in close relationships. *Journal of Social and Personal Relationships, 12*, 547–552.

Baldwin, M. W., & Holmes, J. G. (1987). Salient private audiences and awareness of the self. *Journal of Personality and Social Psychology, 52*, 1087–1098.

Basow, S. A. (1992). *Gender stereotypes* (3rd ed.). Monterey, CA: Brooks/Cole.

Bauserman, R. (1996). Sexual aggression and pornography: A review of correlational research. *Basic and Applied Social Psychology, 18*, 405–427.

Beall, A. E., & Sternberg, R. J. (1995). The social construction of love. *Journal of Social and Personal Relationships, 12*, 417–438.

Becker, M. H., & Joseph, J. G. (1988). AIDS and behavioral change to reduce risk: A review. *American Journal of Public Health, 78*, 394–410.

Bem, D. J. (1996). Exotic becomes erotic: A developmental theory of sexual orientation. *Psychological Review, 103*, 320–335.

Berenbaum, S. A., & Snyder, E. (1995). Early hormonal influences on childhood sex-typed activity and playmate preferences: Implications for the development of sexual orientation. *Developmental Psychology, 31*, 31–42.

Berk, R., Abramson, P. R., & Okami, P. (1995). Sexual activities as told in surveys. In P. R. Abramson & S. D. Pinkerton (Eds.), *Sexual nature, sexual culture* (pp. 371–386). Chicago: University of Chicago Press.

Berliner, L., & Conte, J. R. (1993). Sexual abuse evaluations: Conceptual and empirical obstacles. *Child Abuse & Neglect, 17*, 111–125.

Binson, D., & Catania, J. A. (1998). Respondents' understanding of the words used in sexual behavior questions. *Public Opinion Quarterly, 62*, 190–208.

Blair, J. (1999). A probability sample of gay urban males: The use of two-phase adaptive sampling. *The Journal of Sex Research, 36*, 39–44.

Blinn-Pike, L. (1999). Why abstinent adolescents report they have not had sex: Understanding sexually resilient youth. *Family Relations, 48*, 295–301.

Brannigan, G. C., Allgeier, E. R., & Allgeier, A. R. (1998). *The sex scientists*. New York: Addison-Wesley.

Brecher, E. M., & Brecher, J. (1986). Extracting valid sexological findings from severely flawed and biased population samples. *The Journal of Sex Research, 22*, 6–20.

Brehmer, A., & Brehmer, B. (1988). What have we learned about human judgment from thirty years of policy capturing? In B. Brehmer & C. R. B. Joyce (Eds.), *Human judgment: The SJT view* (pp. 75–114). New York: Elsevier.

Breier, J. (1992). Methodological issues in the study of sexual abuse effects. *Journal of Consulting and Clinical Psychology, 60*, 196–203.

Brock, K. J., Mintz, L. B., & Good, G. E. (1997). Differences among sexually abused and nonabused women from functional and dysfunctional families. *Journal of Counseling Psychology, 44*, 425–432.

Brown, N. R. (1995). Estimation strategies and the judgment of event frequency. *Journal of Experimental Psychology: Learning, Memory, and Cognition, 21*, 1539–1553.

Brown, N. R. (1997). Context memory and the selection of frequency estimation strategies. *Journal of Experimental Psychology: Learning, Memory, and Cognition, 23,* 898–914.

Brown, N. R., & Sinclair, R. C. (1999). Estimating number of lifetime sexual partners: Men and women do it differently. *The Journal of Sex Research, 36,* 292–297.

Bullough, V. L. (1998). Kinsey revisited. *The Journal of Sex Research, 35,* 215–216.

Byers, E. S. (1988). Effects of sexual arousal on men's and women's behavior in sexual disagreement situations. *The Journal of Sex Research, 25,* 235–254.

Byne, W., & Parsons, B. (1993). Human sexual orientation: The biologic theories reappraised. *Archives of General Psychiatry, 50,* 228–239.

Caron, S. L. (1998). *Cross-cultural perspectives on human sexuality.* Boston: Allyn and Bacon.

Caron, S. L., Davis, C. M., Wynn, R. L., & Roberts, L. W. (1992). "America responds to AIDS," but did college students? Differences between March 1987 and September 1988. *AIDS Education and Prevention, 4,* 18–28.

Catania, J. A. (1999). A framework for conceptualizing reporting bias and its antecedents in interviews assessing human sexuality. *The Journal of Sex Research, 36,* 25–38.

Catania, J. A., Binson, D., Canchola, J., Pollack, L. M., Hauck, W., & Coates, T. J. (1996). Effects of interviewer gender, interviewer choice, and item wording on responses to questions concerning sexual behavior. *Public Opinion Quarterly, 60,* 345–375.

Catania, J. A., Turner, H., Pierce, R. C., Golden, E., Stocking, C., Binson, D., & Mast, K. (1993). Response bias in surveys of AIDS-related sexual behavior. In D. G. Ostrow & R. C. Kessler (Eds.), *Methodological issues in AIDS behavioral research* (pp. 133–162). New York: Plenum.

Cecil, H., & Zimet, G. D. (1998). Meanings assigned by undergraduates to frequency statements of condom use. *Archives of Sexual Behavior, 27,* 493–505.

Chara, P. J., & Kuennen, L. M. (1994). Diverging gender attitudes regarding casual sex: A cross-sectional study. *Psychological Reports, 74,* 57–58.

Charny, I. W., & Parnass, S. (1995). The impact of extramarital relationships on the continuation of marriage. *Journal of Sex & Marital Therapy, 21,* 100–115.

Christopher, F. S., & Cate, R. M. (1984). Factors involved in premarital sexual decision-making. *The Journal of Sex Research, 20,* 363–376.

Christopher, F. S., & Cate, R. M. (1985). Premarital sexual pathways and relationship development. *Journal of Social and Personal Relationships, 2,* 271–288.

Chu, J. A., Frey, L. M., Ganzel, B. L., & Matthews, J. A. (1999). Memories of childhood abuse: Dissociation, amnesia, and corroboration. *American Journal of Psychiatry, 156,* 749–755.

Clark, C. L., Shaver, P. R., & Abrahams, M. F. (1999). Strategic behaviors in romantic relationship initiation. *Personality and Social Psychology Bulletin, 25,* 707–720.

Clements, M. (1994, August 7). Sex in America today: A new national survey reveals how our attitudes are changing. *Parade Magazine,* 4–6.

Cohen, G. S., Byrne, C., Hay, J., & Schmuck, M. L. (1996). An 18-month follow-up on the effectiveness of a sexuality workshop: Some methodological pitfalls. *Journal of Sex & Marital Therapy, 22*, 3–8.

Cohen, L. L., & Shotland, R. L. (1996). Timing of first sexual intercourse in a relationship: Expectations, experiences, and perceptions of others. *The Journal of Sex Research, 33*, 291–299.

Conrad, F. G., Brown, N. R., & Cashman, E. R. (1998). Strategies for estimating behavioural frequency in survey interviews. *Memory, 6*, 339–366.

Council, J. R. (1993). Context effects in personality research. *Current Directions in Psychological Science, 2*, 31–34.

Critelli, J. W., & Neumann, K. F. (1984). The placebo: Conceptual analysis of a construct in transition. *American Psychologist, 39*, 32–39.

Croyle, R. T., & Loftus, E. F. (1993). Recollections in the kingdom of AIDS. In D. G. Ostrow & R. C. Kessler (Eds.), *Methodological issues in AIDS behavioral research* (pp. 163–180). New York: Plenum.

Cunningham, J. D., & Antill, J. K. (1994). Cohabitation and marriage: Retrospective and predictive comparisons. *Journal of Social and Personal Relationships, 11*, 77–93.

Davis, C. M., & Bauserman, R. (1993). Exposure to sexually explicit materials: An attitude change perspective. *Annual Review of Sex Research, 4*, 121–209.

Davis, C. M., Yarber, W. L., Bauserman, R., Schreer, G., & Davis, S. L. (Eds.) (1998). *Handbook of sexuality-related measures*. Thousand Oaks, CA: Sage.

Davis, P. J. (1999). Gender differences in autobiographical memory for childhood emotional experiences. *Journal of Personality and Social Psychology, 76*, 498–510.

Dawes, R. M. (1988). *Rational choice in an uncertain world*. New York: Harcourt Brace Jovanovich.

Deal, J. E., & Anderson, E. R. (1995). Reporting and interpreting results in family research. *Journal of Marriage and the Family, 57*, 1040–1048.

DeBuono, B. A., Zinner, S. H., Daamen, M., & McCormack, W. H. (1990). Sexual behavior of college women in 1975, 1986, and 1989. *New England Journal of Medicine, 322*, 821–825.

de Gaston, J. F., Jensen, L., Weed, S. E., & Tanas, R. (1994). Teacher philosophy and program implementation and the impact on sex education outcomes. *Journal of Research and Development in Education, 27*, 265–270.

de Jong Gierveld, J. (1995). Research into relationship research designs: Personal relationships under the microscope. *Journal of Social and Personal Relationships, 12*, 583–588.

DeMaris, A., & Rao, K. V. (1992). Premarital cohabitation and subsequent marital stability in the United States: A reassessment. *Journal of Marriage and the Family, 54*, 178–190.

De Munck, V. C. (Ed.) (1998). *Romantic love and sexual behavior: Perspectives from the social sciences*. Westport, CT: Praeger.

Desrochers, S. (1995). What types of men are most attractive and most repulsive to women? *Sex Roles, 32*, 375–384.

Diamond, M. (1993). Some genetic considerations in the development of sexual orientation. In M. Haug, R. E. Whalen, C. Aron, & K. L. Olsen (Eds.), *The development of
sex differences and similarities in behaviour, Vol. 73* (pp. 291–309). London: Kluwer.

Diamond, M. (1998). Bisexuality: A biological perspective. In E. J. Haeberle & R. Gin-
dorf (Eds.), *Bisexualities* (pp. 53–80). New York: Continuum.

Diamond, M. (1999). The effects of pornography: An international perspective. In J.
Elias, V. Bullough, V. Elias, G. Brewer, J. Douglas, & W. Jarvis (Eds.), *Pornography
101: Eroticism, sexuality and the first amendment* (pp. 225–263). Buffalo, NY:
Prometheus.

Diamond, M., & Uchiyama, A. (1999). Pornography, rape, and sex crimes in Japan. *International Journal of Law and Psychiatry, 22*, 1–22.

Donald, M., Lucke, J., Dunne, M., & Raphael, B. (1995). Gender differences associated
with young people's emotional reactions to sexual intercourse. *Journal of Youth and
Adolescence, 24*, 453–464.

Downey, L., Ryan, R., Roffman, R., & Kulich, M. (1995). How could I forget? Inaccurate
memories of sexually intimate moments. *The Journal of Sex Research, 32*, 177–191.

Dunne, M. P., Martin, N. G., Statham, D. J., Pangan, T., Madden, P. A., & Heath, A. C.
(1997). The consistency of recalled age at first sexual intercourse. *Journal of Biosocial Science, 29*, 1–7.

Dynarski, M. (1997). Trade-offs in designing a social program experiment. *Children and
Youth Services Review, 19*, 525–540.

Ellis, B. J., & Symons, D. (1990). Sex differences in sexual fantasy: An evolutionary psychological approach. *The Journal of Sex Research, 27*, 527–555.

Ellis, L., & Ames, M. A. (1987). Neurohormonal functioning and sexual orientation: A
theory of homosexuality-heterosexuality. *Psychological Bulletin, 10*, 233–258.

Ellis, L., & Ebertz, L. (Eds.) (1997). *Sexual orientation: Toward biological understanding.*
Westport, CT: Praeger.

Ezeh, A. C., & Mboup, G. (1997). Estimates and explanations of gender differences in
contraceptive prevalence rates. *Studies in Family Planning, 28*, 104–121.

Feldman, S. S., Turner, R. A., & Araujo, K. (1999). Interpersonal context as an influence
on sexual timetables of youths: Gender and ethnic effects. *Journal of Research on
Adolescence, 9*, 25–52.

Fergusson, D. M. (1999). *Child sexual abuse.* Thousand Oaks, CA: Sage.

Fisher, T. D., & Alexander, M. G. (1999, May). *Sex differences in reports of masturbation
as function of testing conditions.* Paper presented at the Annual Conference of the
Midcontinent Region of the Society for the Scientific Study of Sexuality, Madison,
WI.

Fisher, W. A., & Grenier, G. (1994). Violent pornography, antiwoman thoughts, and antiwoman effects: In search of reliable effects. *The Journal of Sex Research, 31*, 23–38.

Fletcher, G. J. O., Simpson, J. A., Thomas, G., & Giles, L., (1999). Ideals in intimate relationships. *Journal of Personality and Social Psychology, 76*, 72–89.

Forste, R., & Tanfer, K. (1996). Sexual exclusivity among dating, cohabiting, and married
women. *Journal of Marriage and the Family, 58*, 33–47.

Frable, D. E. S., Johnson, A. E., & Kellman, H. (1997). Seeing masculine men, sexy
women, and gender differences: Exposure to pornography and cognitive constructions of gender. *Journal of Personality, 65*, 311–355.

Friedman, W. J. (1993). Memory for the time of past events. *Psychological Bulletin, 113,* 44–66.

Geer, J. H. (1996). Gender differences in the organization of sexual information. *Archives of Sexual Behavior, 25,* 91–107.

Gidycz, C. A., Hanson, K., & Layman, M. J. (1995). A prospective analysis of the relationships among sexual assault experiences: An extension of previous findings. *Psychology of Women Quarterly, 19,* 5–29.

Gladstone, G., Parker, G., Wilhelm, K., Mitchell, P., & Austin, M. (1999). Characteristics of depressed patients who report childhood sexual abuse. *American Journal of Psychiatry, 156,* 431–437.

Gladue, B. A. (1994). The biopsychology of sexual orientation. *Current Directions in Psychological Science, 3,* 150–154.

Glass, S. P., & Wright, T. L. (1992). Justifications for extramarital relationships: The association between attitudes, behaviors, and gender. *The Journal of Sex Research, 29,* 361–387.

Goleman, D. (1995). *Emotional intelligence.* New York: Bantam.

Gribble, J. N., Miller, H. G., Rogers, S. M., & Turner, C. F. (1999). Interview mode and measurement of sexual behaviors: Methodological issues. *The Journal of Sex Research, 36,* 16–24.

Grober, M. S. (1998). Socially controlled sex change: Integrating ultimate and proximate levels of analysis. *Acta Ethological, 1,* 3–17.

Grote, N. K., & Frieze, I. H. (1998). "Remembrance of things past": Perceptions of marital love from its beginning to the present. *Journal of Social and Personal Relationships, 15,* 91–109.

Groves, R. M., Cialdini, R. B., & Couper, M. P. (1992). Understanding the decision to participate in a survey. *Public Opinion Quarterly, 56,* 475–495.

Grunseit, A., Kippax, S., Aggleton, P., Baldo, M., & Slutkin, G. (1997). Sexuality education and young people's sexual behavior: A review of studies. *Journal of Adolescent Research, 12,* 421–453.

Gunthar, A. C. (1995). Overrating the X-rating: The third-person perception and support for censorship of pornography. *Journal of Communication, 45,* 27–38.

Guthrie, B. J., Wallace, J., Doerr, K., Janz, N., Schottenfeld, D., & Selig, S. (1996). Girl talk: Development of an intervention for prevention of HIV/AIDS and other sexually transmitted diseases in adolescent females. *Public Health Nursing, 13,* 318–330.

Halpern, D. F. (1998). Teaching critical thinking transfer across domains: Dispositions, skills, structure training, and metacognitive monitoring. *American Psychologist, 53,* 449–455.

Halpern-Flesher, B. L., Millstein, S. G., & Ellen, J. M. (1996). Relationship of alcohol use and risky sexual behavior: A review and analysis of findings. *Journal of Adolescent Health, 19,* 331–336.

Hamer, D., & Copeland, P. (1994). *The science of desire: The search for the gay gene and the biology of behavior.* New York: Simon & Schuster.

Hansen, G. L. (1987). Extradyadic relations during courtship. *The Journal of Sex Research, 23,* 382–390.

Harris, G. T., & Rice, M. E. (1996). The science in phallometric measurement of male sexual interest. *Current Directions in Psychological Science, 5,* 156–160.

Harvey, J. H., Flanary, R., & Morgan, M. (1986). Vivid memories of vivid loves gone by. *Journal of Social and Personal Relationships, 3*, 359–373.

Hatfield, E., & Rapson, R. L. (1987). Passionate love/sexual desire: Can the same paradigm explain both? *Archives of Sexual Behavior, 16*, 259–278.

Hatfield, E., & Rapson, R. L. (1993). *Love, sex, and intimacy: Their psychology, biology, and history*. New York: HarperCollins.

Hatfield, E., & Rapson, R. L. (1996). *Love and sex: Cross-cultural perspectives*. Boston: Allyn and Bacon.

Hatfield, E., & Sprecher, S. (1995). Men's and women's preferences in marital partners in the United States, Russia, and Japan. *Journal of Cross-Cultural Psychology, 26*, 728–750.

Haugaard, J. J. (1996). Sexual behaviors between children: Professionals' opinions and undergraduates' recollections. *Families in Society: The Journal of Contemporary Human Services, 2*, 81–89.

Hazard, W. R., & Einstein, V. (1993). Legal aspects of sex education: Implications for school administrators. *Journal of Research and Development in Education, 16*, 34–40.

Heiman, M. L., Leiblum, S., Esquilin, S. C., & Pallitto, L. M. (1998). A comparative survey of beliefs about "normal" childhood sexual behaviors. *Child Abuse & Neglect, 22*, 289–304.

Hencken, J. D. (1984). Conceptualizations of homosexual behavior which preclude homosexual self-labeling. *Journal of Homosexuality, 9*(4), 53–63.

Henry, B., Moffitt, T. E., Caspi, A., Langley, J., & Silva, P. A. (1994). On the "remembrance of things past": A longitudinal evaluation of the retrospective method. *Psychological Assessment, 6*, 92–101.

Herold, E. S., & Milhausen, R. R. (1999). Dating preferences of university women: An analysis of the nice guy stereotype. *Journal of Sex & Marital Therapy, 25*, 333–343.

Hewitt, C. (1998). Homosexual demography: Implications for the spread of AIDS. *The Journal of Sex Research, 35*, 390–396.

Hite, S. (1976). *The Hite report*. New York: Dell.

Hite, S. (1983). *The Hite report on male sexuality*. New York: Knopf.

Holmes, G. R., Offen, L., & Waller, G. (1997). See no evil, hear no evil, speak no evil: Why do relatively few male victims of childhood sexual abuse receive help for abuse-related issues in adulthood? *Clinical Psychology Review, 17*, 69–88.

Horvath, P. (1988). Placebos and common factors in two decades of psychotherapy research. *Psychological Bulletin, 104*, 214–225.

Hunt, M. (1974). *Sexual behavior in the 1970s*. Chicago: Playboy Press.

Huygens, P., Kajura, E., Seeley, J., & Barton, T. (1996). Rethinking methods for the study of sexual behaviour. *Social Science and Medicine, 42*, 221–231.

Hyde, J. S. (1994). Can meta-analysis make feminist transformations in psychology? *Psychology of Women Quarterly, 18*, 451–462.

Ishii-Kuntz, M., Whitbeck, L. B., & Simons, R. L. (1990). AIDS and perceived change in sexual practice: An analysis of a college student sample from California and Iowa. *Journal of Applied Social Psychology, 20*, 1301–1321.

Jaccard, J., & Wan, C. K. (1995). A paradigm for studying the accuracy of self-reports of risk behavior relevant to AIDS: Empirical perspectives on stability, recall bias, and transitory influences. *Journal of Applied Social Psychology, 25*, 1831–1858.

Jasso, G. (1985). Marital coital frequency and the passage of time: Estimating the separate effects of spouses' ages and marital duration, birth and marriage cohorts, and period influences. *American Sociological Review, 50*, 224–241.

Jeannin, A., Konings, E., Dubois-Arber, F., Landert, C., & Van Melle, G. (1998). Validity and reliability in reporting sexual partners and condom use in a Swiss population survey. *European Journal of Epidemiology, 14*, 139–146.

Jenks, R. J. (1998). Swinging: A review of the literature. *Archives of Sexual Behavior, 27*, 507–521.

Jones, J. C., & Barlow, D. H. (1990). Self-reported frequency of sexual urges, fantasies, and masturbatory fantasies in heterosexual males and females. *Archives of Sexual Behavior, 19*, 269–279.

Jones, J. H. (1997). *Alfred C. Kinsey: A public/private life*. New York: W. W. Norton.

Jurich, J. A., Adams, R. A., & Schulenberg, J. E. (1992). Factors related to behavior change in response to AIDS. *Family Relations, 41*, 97–103.

Kane, E. W., & Schippers, M. (1996). Men's and women's beliefs about gender and sexuality. *Gender & Society, 10*, 650–665.

Kaplan, H. B. (1989). Methodological problems in the study of psychosocial influences on the AIDS process. *Social Science and Medicine, 29*, 277–292.

Karney, B. R., Davila, J., Cohan, C. L., Sullivan, K. T., Johnson, M. D., & Bradbury, T. N. (1995). An empirical investigation of sampling strategies in marital research. *Journal of Marriage and the Family, 57*, 909–920.

Kendall-Tackett, K. A., Williams, L. M., & Finkelhor, D. (1993). Impact of sexual abuse on children: A review and synthesis of recent empirical studies. *Psychological Bulletin, 113*, 164–180.

Kimmel, M. S., & Linders, A. (1996). Does censorship make a difference? An aggregate empirical analysis of pornography and rape. *Journal of Psychology and Human Sexuality, 8*(3), 1–20.

Kinsey, A. C., Pomeroy, W. B., & Martin, C. E. (1948). *Sexual behavior in the human male*. Philadelphia: Saunders.

Kinsey, A. C., Pomeroy, W. B., Martin, C. E., & Gebhard, P. H. (1953). *Sexual behavior in the human female*. Philadelphia: Saunders.

Kirby, D., & Coyle, K. (1997). School-based programs to reduce sexual risk-taking behavior. *Children and Youth Services Review, 19*, 415–436.

Kirk, K. M., Bailey, J. M., & Martin, N. G. (1999). How accurate is the family history method for assessing siblings' sexual orientation? *Archives of Sexual Behavior, 28*, 129–137.

Kisker, E. E., & Brown, R. S. (1997). Nonexperimental designs and program evaluation. *Children and Youth Services Review, 19*, 541–556.

Kitzinger, C., & Wilkinson, S. (1995). Transitions from heterosexuality to lesbianism: The discursive production of lesbian identities. *Developmental Psychology, 31*, 95–104.

Knee, C. R. (1998). Implicit theories of relationships: Assessment and prediction of romantic relationship initiation, coping, and longevity. *Journal of Personality and Social Psychology, 74*, 360–370.

Kupek, E. (1998). Determinants of item nonresponse in a large national sex survey. *Archives of Sexual Behavior, 27*, 581–594.

Kyman, W. (1998). Into the 21st century: Renewing the campaign for school-based sexuality education. *Journal of Sex & Marital Therapy, 24*, 131–137.

Lamb, S., & Coakley, M. (1993). "Normal" childhood sexual play and games: Differentiating play from abuse. *Child Abuse & Neglect, 17*, 515–526.

Lamm, H., Wiesmann, U., & Keller, K. (1998). Subjective determinants of attraction: Self-perceived causes of the rise and decline of liking, love, and being in love. *Personal Relationships, 5*, 91–104.

LaRossa, R. (1995). Stories and relationships. *Journal of Social and Personal Relationships, 12*, 553–558.

Laumann, E. O., Gagnon, J. H., Michael, R. T., & Michaels, S. (1994). *The social organization of sexuality: Sexual practices in the United States*. Chicago: University of Chicago Press.

Laumann, E. O., Paik, A., & Rosen, R. C. (1999). Sexual dysfunction in the United States: Prevalence and predictors. *JAMA: Journal of the American Medical Association, 281*, 537–544.

Lauritsen, J. L., & Swicegood, C. G. (1997). The consistency of self-reported initiation of sexual activity. *Family Planning Perspectives, 29*, 215–221.

Leitenberg, H., & Henning, K. (1995). Sexual fantasy. *Psychological Bulletin, 117*, 469–496.

LeVay, S. (1996). *Queer science: The use and abuse of research into homosexuality*. Cambridge, MA: MIT Press.

Levine, S. B. (1998). Extramarital sexual affairs. *Journal of Sex & Marital Therapy, 24*, 207–216.

Lewinsohn, P. M., & Rosenbaum, M. (1987). Recall of parental behavior by acute depressives, remitted depressives, and nondepressives. *Journal of Personality and Social Psychology, 52*, 611–619.

Lewis, J. E., Malow, R. M., & Ireland, S. (1997). HIV/AIDS risk in heterosexual college students: A review of a decade of literature. *American Journal of College Student Health, 45*, 147–158.

Lewontin, R. C. (1995). Sex, lies, and social science. *The Public Perspective, 6*(4), 4–6.

Lief, H. I., & Fetkewicz, J. (1995). Retractors of false memories: The evolution of pseudomemories. *Journal of Psychiatry & Law, 23*, 411–435.

Loftus, E. F., Garry, M., & Feldman, J. (1994). Forgetting sexual trauma: What does it mean when 38% forget? *Journal of Consulting and Clinical Psychology, 62*, 1177–1181.

Loftus, E. F., & Ketcham, K. (1994). *The myth of repressed memory*. New York: St. Martin's Press.

Loftus, E. F., & Pickrell, J. E. (1995). The formation of false memories. *Psychiatric Annals, 25*, 720–725.

Malamuth, N. M. (1996). Sexually explicit media, gender, and evolutionary theory. *Journal of Communication, 46*, 8–31.

Marsh, H. W., & Yeung, A. S. (1999). The lability of psychological ratings: The chameleon effect in global self-esteem. *Personality and Social Psychology Bulletin, 25*, 49–64.

Marston, P. J., Hecht, M. L., Manke, M. L., McDaniel, S., & Reeder, H. (1998). The subjective experience of intimacy, passion, and commitment in heterosexual loving relationships. *Personal Relationships, 5*, 15–30.

Masters, W. H., & Johnson, V. E. (1970). *Human sexual inadequacy.* Boston: Little, Brown.

Maticka-Tyndale, E., & Herold, E. S. (1997). The scripting of sexual behaviour: Canadian university students on spring break in Florida. *Canadian Journal of Human Sexuality, 6*, 317–328.

Maynard, C., & Wiederman, M. W. (1997). Undergraduate students' perceptions of child sexual abuse: Effects of age, sex, and gender-role attitudes. *Child Abuse & Neglect, 21*, 833–844.

McClelland, D. C. (1986). Some reflections on the two psychologies of love. *Journal of Personality, 54*, 334–353.

McClintock, M. K., & Herdt, G. (1996). Rethinking puberty: The development of sexual attraction. *Current Directions in Psychological Science, 5*, 178–183.

McFarland, C., & Ross, M. (1987). The relation between current impressions and memories of self and dating partners. *Personality and Social Psychology Bulletin, 13*, 228–238.

McGregor, I., & Holmes, J. G. (1999). How storytelling shapes memory and impressions of relationship events over time. *Journal of Personality and Social Psychology, 76*, 403–419.

McKay, A., Pietrusiak, M. A., & Hollowaty, P. (1998). Parents' opinions and attitudes toward sexuality education in the schools. *Canadian Journal of Human Sexuality, 7*, 139–145.

Melnick, S. L., Jeffery, R. W., Burke, G. L., Gilbertson, D. T., Perkins, L. L., Sidney, S., McCreath, H. E., Wagenknecht, L. E., & Hulley, S. B. (1993). Changes in sexual behavior by young urban heterosexual adults in response to the AIDS epidemic. *Public Health Reports, 108*, 582–588.

Messman, T. L., & Long, P. J. (1996). Child sexual abuse and its relationship to revictimization in adult women: A review. *Clinical Psychology Review, 16*, 397–420.

Moeller, T. P., Bachman, G. A., & Moeller, J. R. (1993). The combined effects of physical, sexual, and emotional abuse during childhood: Long-term health consequences for women. *Child Abuse & Neglect, 17*, 623–640.

Morrow, G. D., Clark, E. M., & Brock, K. F. (1995). Individual and partner love styles: Implications for the quality of romantic involvement. *Journal of Social and Personal Relationships, 12*, 363–387.

Murray, S. L., Holmes, J. G., & Griffin, D. W. (1996). The self-fulfilling nature of positive illusions in romantic relationships: Love is not blind, but prescient. *Journal of Personality and Social Psychology, 71*, 1155–1180.

Myers, S. A., & Berscheid, E. (1997). The language of love: The difference a preposition makes. *Personality and Social Psychology Bulletin, 23*, 347–362.

National Institute of Mental Health (NIMH) Multisite HIV Prevention Trial Group (1998). The NIMH multisite HIV prevention trial: Reducing HIV sexual risk behavior. *Science, 280*, 1889–1894.

Nicholas, L. J., Durrheim, K., & Tredoux, C. G. (1994). Lying as a factor in research on sexuality. *Psychological Reports, 75*, 839–842.

Nisbett, R. E., & Ross, L. (1980). *Human inference: Strategies and shortcomings of social judgment.* Englewood Cliffs, NJ: Prentice-Hall.

Nisbett, R. E., & Wilson, T. D. (1977). Telling more than we can know: Verbal reports on mental processes. *Psychological Review, 84,* 231–259.

Okami, P., Olmstead, R., & Abramson, P. R. (1997). Sexual experiences in early childhood: 18-year longitudinal data from the UCLA Family Lifestyles Project. *The Journal of Sex Research, 34,* 339–347.

Oliver, M. B., & Hyde, J. S. (1993). Gender differences in sexuality: A meta-analysis. *Psychological Bulletin, 114,* 29–51.

Ottati, V. C. (1997). When the survey question directs retrieval: Implications for assessing the cognitive and affective predictors of global evaluation. *European Journal of Social Psychology, 27,* 1–21.

Paik, H., & Comstock, G. (1994). The effects of television violence on antisocial behavior: A meta-analysis. *Communication Research, 21,* 516–546.

Penn, C. D., Hernandez, S. L., & Bermudez, J. M. (1997). Using a cross-cultural perspective to understand infidelity in couples therapy. *Journal of Sex & Marital Therapy, 23,* 169–185.

Pennebaker, J. W. (1997). Writing about emotional experiences as a therapeutic process. *Psychological Science, 8,* 162–166.

Plaud, J. J., Gaither, G. A., Hegstad, H. J., Rowan, L., & Devitt, M. K. (1999). Volunteer bias in human psychophysiological sexual arousal research: To whom do our research results apply? *The Journal of Sex Research, 36,* 171–179.

Plummer, K. (1995). *Telling sexual stories: Power, change and social worlds.* New York: Routledge.

Polusny, M. A., & Follette, V. M. (1995). Long-term correlates of childhood sexual abuse: Theory and review of the empirical literature. *Applied & Preventive Psychology, 4,* 143–166.

Pope, H. G., Jr. (1997). *Psychology astray: Fallacies in studies of "repressed memory" and childhood trauma.* Boca Raton, FL: Upton Books.

Poppen, P. J., & Reisen, C. A. (1997). Perception of risk and sexual self-protective behavior: A methodological critique. *AIDS Education and Prevention, 9,* 373–390.

Poulson, R. L., Eppler, M. A., Satterwhite, T. N., Wuensch, K. L., & Bass, L. A. (1998). Alcohol consumption, strength of religious beliefs and risky sexual behavior in college students. *Journal of American College Health, 46,* 227–232.

Prentice, D. A., & Miller, D. T. (1992). When small effects are impressive. *Psychological Bulletin, 112,* 160–164.

Quitkin, F. M. (1999). Placebos, drug effects, and study design: A clinician's guide. *American Journal of Psychiatry, 156,* 829–836.

Raghubir, P., & Menon, G. (1996). Asking sensitive questions: The effects of type of referent and frequency wording in counterbiasing methods. *Psychology & Marketing, 13,* 633–652.

Regan, P. C. (1998). Romantic love and sexual desire. In V. C. De Munck (Ed.), *Romantic love and sexual behavior: Perspectives from the social sciences* (pp. 91–132). Westport, CT: Praeger.

Regan, P. C., & Berscheid, E. (1996). Beliefs about the state, goals, and objects of sexual desire. *Journal of Sex & Marital Therapy, 22,* 110–120.

Regan, P. C., Kocan, E. R., & Whitlock, T. (1998). Ain't love grand! A prototype analysis of the concept of romantic love. *Journal of Social and Personal Relationships, 15,* 411–420.

Reiss, I. L., & Leik, R. K. (1989). Evaluating strategies to avoid AIDS: Number of partners vs. use of condoms. *The Journal of Sex Research, 26,* 411–433.

Rind, B. (1995). An analysis of human sexuality textbook coverage of the psychological correlates of adult-nonadult sex. *The Journal of Sex Research, 32,* 219–233.

Rind, B., & Bauserman, R. (1993). Biased terminology effects and biased information processing in research on adult-nonadult sexual interactions: An empirical investigation. *The Journal of Sex Research, 30,* 260–269.

Rind, B., & Tromovitch, P. (1997). A meta-analytic review of findings from national samples on psychological correlates of child sexual abuse. *The Journal of Sex Research, 34,* 237–255.

Rind, B., Tromovitch, P., & Bauserman, R. (1998). A meta-analytic examination of assumed properties of child sexual abuse using college samples. *Psychological Bulletin, 124,* 22–53.

Robinson, J., & Godbey, G. (1998). No sex please . . . we're college graduates. *American Demographics, 20*(2), 18–23.

Roosa, M. W., Reyes, L., Reinholtz, C., & Angelini, P. J. (1998). Measurement of women's child sexual abuse experiences: An empirical demonstration of the impact of choice of measure on estimates of incidence rates and of relationships with pathology. *The Journal of Sex Research, 35,* 225–233.

Roscoe, B., Cavanaugh, L. E., & Kennedy, D. R. (1988). Dating infidelity: Behaviors, reasons and consequences. *Adolescence, 23,* 35–43.

Rosen, R. C., & Leiblum, S. R. (1995). Treatment of sexual disorders in the 1990s: An integrated approach. *Journal of Consulting and Clinical Psychology, 63,* 877–890.

Rosenbluth, S. (1997). Is sexual orientation a matter of choice? *Psychology of Women Quarterly, 21,* 595–610.

Rosenthal, D., Fernbach, M., & Moore, S. (1997). The singles scene: Safe sex practices and attitudes among at-risk heterosexual adults. *Psychology and Health, 12,* 171–182.

Rosenthal, R. (1994). Science and ethics in conducting, analyzing, and reporting psychological research. *Psychological Science, 5,* 127–134.

Rosenthal, R., & Rosnow, R. L. (1991). *Essentials of behavioral research: Methods and data analysis* (2nd ed.). New York: McGraw-Hill.

Rosnow, R. L., & Rosenthal, R. (1996). Computing contrasts, effects sizes, and counternulls on other people's published data: General procedures for research consumers. *Psychological Methods, 1,* 331–340.

Rosnow, R. L., & Rosenthal, R. (1999). *Beginning behavioral research: A conceptual primer* (3rd ed.). Upper Saddle River, NJ: Prentice Hall.

Ross, R., & Allgeier, E. R. (1996). Behind the pencil/paper measurement of sexual coercion: Interview-based clarification of men's interpretations of Sexual Experience Survey items. *Journal of Applied Social Psychology, 26,* 1587–1616.

Rothblum, E. D. (1994). Transforming lesbian sexuality. *Psychology of Women Quarterly, 18,* 627–641.

Rottnek, M. (Ed.) (1999). *Sissies and tomboys: Gender nonconformity and homosexual childhood*. New York: New York University Press.

Rowland, D. L. (1999). Issues in the laboratory study of human sexual response: A synthesis for the nontechnical sexologist. *The Journal of Sex Research, 36*, 3–15.

Russell, D. E. H. (1998). *Dangerous relationships: Pornography, misogyny, and rape*. Thousand Oaks, CA: Sage.

Sanders, S. A., & Reinisch, J. M. (1999). Would you say you "had sex" if . . . ? *JAMA: Journal of the American Medical Association, 281*, 275–277.

Sandfort, T. G. M. (1997). Sampling male homosexuality. In J. Bancroft (Ed.), *Researching sexual behavior* (pp. 261–275). Bloomington, IN: Indiana University Press.

Schuklenk, U., & Ristow, M. (1996). The ethics of research into the cause(s) of homosexuality. *Journal of Homosexuality, 31*(3), 5–30.

Schwartz, N. (1999). Self-reports: How the questions shape the answers. *American Psychologist, 54*, 93–105.

Schwartz, P., & Rutter, V. (1998). *The gender of sexuality*. Thousand Oaks, CA: Pine Forge Press.

Sedikides, C., Oliver, M. B., & Campbell, W. K. (1994). Perceived benefits and costs of romantic relationships for women and men: Implications for exchange theory. *Personal Relationships, 1*, 5–21.

Seidman, S. (1991). *Romantic longings: Love in America, 1830–1980*. New York: Routledge.

Seidman, S. N., & Rieder, R. O. (1994). A review of sexual behavior in the United States. *American Journal of Psychiatry, 151*, 330–341.

Sell, R. L. (1997). Defining and measuring sexual orientation: A review. *Archives of Sexual Behavior, 26*, 643–658.

Shackelford, T. K. (1998). Divorce as a consequence of spousal infidelity. In V. C. De Munck (Ed.), *Romantic love and sexual behavior: Perspectives from the social sciences* (pp. 135–153). Westport, CT: Praeger.

Sheeran, P., & Abraham, C. (1994). Measurement of condom use in 72 studies of HIV–preventive behaviour: A critical review. *Patient Education and Counseling, 24*, 199–216.

Sheeran, P., Abraham, C., & Orbell, S. (1999). Psychosocial correlates of heterosexual condom use: A meta-analysis. *Psychological Bulletin, 125*, 90–132.

Sheppard, V. J., Nelson, E. S., & Andreoli-Mathie, V. (1995). Dating relationships and infidelity: Attitudes and behaviors. *Journal of Sex & Marital Therapy, 21*, 202–212.

Siegel, D. M., Aten, M. J., & Roughman, K. J. (1998). Self-reported honesty among middle and high school students responding to a sexual behavior questionnaire. *Journal of Adolescent Health, 23*, 20–28.

Sonenstein, F. L. (1997). Using self reports to measure program impact. *Children and Youth Services Review, 19*, 567–585.

Spector, I. P., & Carey, M. P. (1990). Incidence and prevalence of sexual dysfunctions: A critical review of the empirical literature. *Archives of Sexual Behavior, 19*, 389–408.

Sprecher, S. (1999). "I love you more today than yesterday": Romantic partners' perceptions of changes in love and related affect over time. *Journal of Personality and Social Psychology, 76*, 46–53.

Sprey, J. (1995). Explanatory practice in family studies. *Journal of Marriage and the Family, 57,* 867–878.

Sternberg, R. J. (1995). Love as a story. *Journal of Social and Personal Relationships, 12,* 541–546.

Tanfer, K., Cubbins, L. A., & Billy, J. O. G. (1995). Gender, race, class, and self-reported transmitted disease incidence. *Family Planning Perspectives, 27,* 196–202.

Taris, T. W., & Semin, G. R. (1997). Gender as a moderator of the effects of the love motive and relational context on sexual experience. *Archives of Sexual Behavior, 26,* 159–180.

Tavris, C., & Sadd, S. (1975). *The Redbook report on female sexuality.* New York: Delacorte.

Thompson, A. P. (1983). Extramarital sex: A review of the research literature. *The Journal of Sex Research, 19,* 1–22.

Thompson, B., & Borrello, G. M. (1992). Different views of love: Deductive and inductive lines of inquiry. *Current Directions in Psychological Science, 1,* 154–156.

Tourangeau, R., Smith, T. W., & Rasinski, K. A. (1997). Motivation to report sensitive behaviors on surveys: Evidence from a bogus pipeline experiment. *Journal of Applied Social Psychology, 27,* 209–222.

Townsend, J. M. (1995). Sex without emotional involvement: An evolutionary interpretation of sex differences. *Archives of Sexual Behavior, 24,* 173–204.

Tsui, L. (1999). Courses and instruction affecting critical thinking. *Research in Higher Education, 40,* 185–194.

Turner, C. F., Danella, R. D., & Rogers, S. M. (1995). Sexual behavior in the United States, 1930–1990: Trends and methodological problems. *Sexually Transmitted Diseases, 22,* 173–190.

Turner, C. F., Ku, L., Rogers, S. M., Lindberg, L. D., Pleck, J. H., & Sonenstein, F. L. (1998). Adolescent sexual behavior, drug use, and violence: Increased reporting with computer survey technology. *Science, 280,* 867–873.

Udry, J. R., Deven, F. R., & Coleman, S. J. (1982). A cross-national comparison of the relative influence of male and female age on the frequency of marital intercourse. *Journal of Biosocial Science, 14,* 1–6.

Urquiza, A. J., & Goodlin-Jones, B. L. (1994). Child sexual abuse and adult revictimization with women of color. *Violence and Victims, 9,* 223–232.

Wadsworth, J., Johnson, A. M., Wellings, K., & Field, J. (1996). What's in a mean?—an examination of the inconsistency between men and women in reporting sexual partnerships. *Journal of the Royal Statistical Society, 159,* 111–123.

Weeks, K., Levy, S. R., Gordon, A. K., Handler, A., Perhats, C., & Flay, B. R. (1997). Does parental involvement make a difference? The impact of parent interactive activities on students in a school-based AIDS prevention program. *AIDS Education and Prevention, 9* (Suppl. A), 90–106.

Weinhardt, L. S., Forsyth, A. D., Carey, M. P., Jaworski, B. C., & Durant, L. E. (1998). Reliability and validity of self-report measures of HIV-related sexual behavior: Progress since 1990 and recommendations for research and practice. *Archives of Sexual Behavior, 27,* 155–180.

Weir, S. S., Roddy, R. E., Zekeng, L., Ryan, K. A., & Wong, E. L. (1998). Measuring condom use: Asking "do you or don't you" isn't enough. *AIDS Education and Prevention, 10,* 293–302.

Weiss, E. L., Longhurst, J. G., & Mazure, C. M. (1999). Childhood sexual abuse as a risk factor for depression in women: Psychosocial and neurobiological correlates. *American Journal of Psychiatry, 156,* 816–828.

Wheeler, J., & Kilmann, P. R. (1983). Comarital sexual behavior: Individual and relationship variables. *Archives of Sexual Behavior, 12,* 295–306.

Wiederman, M. W. (1993). Demographic and sexual characteristics of nonresponders to sexual experience items in a national survey. *The Journal of Sex Research, 30,* 27–35.

Wiederman, M. W. (1997a). Extramarital sex: Prevalence and correlates in a national survey. *The Journal of Sex Research, 34,* 167–174.

Wiederman, M. W. (1997b). The truth must be in here somewhere: Examining the gender discrepancy in self-reported lifetime number of sex partners. *The Journal of Sex Research, 34,* 375–386.

Wiederman, M. W. (1998). The state of theory in sex therapy. *The Journal of Sex Research, 35,* 88–99.

Wiederman, M. W. (1999a). Sexuality research, subject pools, and institutional review boards. In G. Chastain & R. E. Landrum (Eds.), *Protecting human subjects: Departmental subject pools and institutional review boards* (pp. 201–219). Washington, DC: American Psychological Association.

Wiederman, M. W. (1999b). Volunteer bias in sexuality research using college student participants. *The Journal of Sex Research, 36,* 59–66.

Wiederman, M. W., & Allgeier, E. R. (1992). Gender differences in mate selection criteria: Sociobiological or socioeconomic explanation? *Ethology and Sociobiology, 13,* 115–124.

Wiederman, M. W., & Allgeier, E. R. (1993). Gender differences in sexual jealousy: Adaptionist or social learning explanation? *Ethology and Sociobiology, 14,* 115–140.

Wiederman, M. W., & Allgeier, E. R. (1996). Expectations and attributions regarding extramarital sex among young married individuals. *Journal of Psychology and Human Sexuality, 8,* 21–35.

Wiederman, M. W., & Dubois, S. L. (1998). Evolution and sex differences in preferences for short-term mates: Results from a policy capturing study. *Evolution and Human Behavior, 19,* 153–170.

Wiederman, M. W., & Hurd, C. (1999). Extradyadic involvement during dating. *Journal of Social and Personal Relationships, 16,* 265–274.

Wiederman, M. W., Maynard, C., & Fretz, A. (1996). Ethnicity in 25 years of published sexuality research: 1971–1995. *The Journal of Sex Research, 33,* 339–342.

Wiederman, M. W., & Whitley, B. E., Jr. (Eds.) (in press). *Handbook for conducting research on human sexuality.* Mahwah, NJ: Erlbaum Associates.

Williams, L. M. (1994). Recall of childhood trauma: A prospective study of women's memories of child sexual abuse. *Journal of Consulting and Clinical Psychology, 62,* 1167–1176.

Williams, M. B. (1993). Assessing the traumatic impact of child sexual abuse: What makes it more severe? *Journal of Child Sexual Abuse, 2*(2), 41–59.

Wilson, T. D., & Stone, J. I. (1985). Limitations of self-knowledge: More on telling more than we can know. *Review of Personality and Social Psychology, 6,* 167–183.

Wind, T. W., & Silvern, L. (1992). Type and extent of child abuse as predictors of adult functioning. *Journal of Family Violence, 7,* 261–281.

Winick, C., & Evans, J. T. (1996). The relationship between nonenforcement of state pornography laws and rates of sex crime arrests. *Archives of Sexual Behavior, 25,* 439–453.

Wortley, P. M., & Fleming, P. L. (1997). AIDS in women in the United States. *JAMA: Journal of the American Medical Association, 278,* 911–916.

Wright, D. B., Gaskell, G. D., & O'Muircheartaigh, C. A. (1997). How response alternatives affect different kinds of behavioural frequency questions. *British Journal of Social Psychology, 36,* 443–456.

Wright, D. E. (1999). *Personal relationships: An interdisciplinary approach.* Mountain View, CA: Mayfield.

Yarab, P. E., Sensibaugh, C. C., & Allgeier, E. R. (1998). More than just sex: Gender differences in the incidence of self-defined unfaithful behavior in heterosexual dating relationships. *Journal of Psychology and Human Sexuality, 10,* 45–57.

Zillman, D., & Weaver, J. B. (1999). Effects of prolonged exposure to gratuitous media violence on provoked and unprovoked hostile behavior. *Journal of Applied Social Psychology, 29,* 145–165.